MOMSTERS

Mothers Who Kill Their Children

Written By

David Pietras
All Rights Reserved
Copyright © 2014

Copyright © 2014 by David J. Pietras

http://mrdavepp.wix.com/davidpietras

Cover design by David Pietras

ISBN-13: 978-1494900212

ISBN-10: 1494900211

2 3 4 5 6 7 8 9 10 14

"Mother's love is peace. It need not be acquired, it need not be deserved."

Erich Fromm German born American social Philosopher and Psychoanalyst, 1900-1980

PROLOGUE

When I was first approached about writing stories about children who have been murdered, I didn't think that it would have been a difficult task.

My first book was *"Profiling The Killer of a Childhood Beauty Queen."*

In this book I took a look at the murder of JonBenet Ramsey and profiled her killer.

My second book was *"No Justice For Caylee Anthony."*

In this book I dealt with the case against her mother Casey Anthony, and her not guilty verdict.

This is my 3rd book on the subject of children who have been murdered. And I will say that this book has been very difficult to write. Trying to focus on the story line knowing that these beautiful children were killed by the one person who was supposed to be their protector really bothered me. And to know that these are true crimes, not something made up in Hollywood. So with the ending of this book, I will no longer venture into the world of childhood murders. These are the true stories that I don't wish to write about any longer.

In this book we will look at four mothers who became Monsters and killed their children in the process.

These mothers are:

Andrea Yates

Susan Smith

Diane Downs

Marybeth Tinning

PART ONE

Andrea Yates

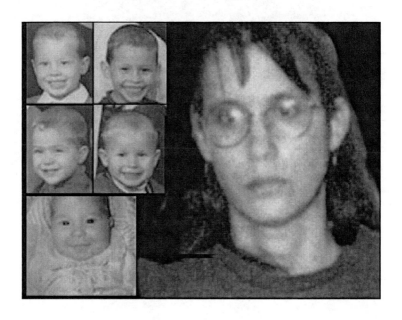

The Call

Around 10:00am on June 20, 2001, Rusty Yates received a startling phone call from his wife, Andrea, whom he had left only an hour before.

"You need to come home," she said.

Puzzled, he asked, "What's going on?"

She just repeated her statement and then added, "It's time. I did it."

Not entirely sure what she meant but in light of her recent illness, he asked her to explain and she said, "It's the children."

Now a chill shot through him. "Which one?" he asked.

"All of them."

He dropped everything and left his job as a NASA engineer at the Johnson Space Center. When he arrived fifteen minutes later, the police and ambulances were already at their Houston, Texas home on the corner of Beachcomber and Sea Lark in the Clear Lake area. Rusty was told he could not go in, so he put his forehead against a brick wall, trying to process the horrifying news, and waited.

Restless for information, he went to a window and on to the back door where he screamed, "How could you do this?" According to an article in *Time*, at one point Rusty Yates collapsed into a fetal position on the lawn, pounding the ground as he watched his wife being led away in handcuffs.

John Cannon, the police spokesperson, described for the media what the team had found.

On a double bed in a back master bedroom, four children were laid out beneath a sheet, clothed and soaking wet. All of them were dead, with their eyes wide open. In the bathtub, a young boy was submerged amid feces and vomit floating on the surface. He looked to be the oldest and he was also dead.

In less than an hour that morning, five children had all been drowned, and the responding officers were deeply affected.

The children's thin, bespectacled mother---the woman who had called 911 seeking help---appeared able to talk coherently, but her frumpy striped shirt and stringy brown hair were soaked. She let the officers in, told them without emotion that she had killed her children, and sat down while they checked. Detective Ed Mehl thought she seemed focused when he asked her questions. She told him she was a bad mother and expected to be punished. Then she allowed the police to take her into custody while medical personnel checked the children for any sign of life. She looked dispassionately at the gathering crowd of curious neighbors as she got into the police car.

Everyone who entered the Spanish-style home could see the little school desks in one room where the woman apparently home-schooled them. The house was cluttered and dirty, with used dishes sitting around in the kitchen. The bathroom was a mess.

Yates' family photo

This crime story would unravel in dark and strange ways, with the reasons why a loving mother of five had drowned all of her children tangled in issues of depression, religious fanaticism, and psychosis. The nation would watch with polarized opinions, as the State of Texas was forced into a determination about justice that was rooted in glaringly outdated ideas about mental illness.

But in the meantime, Andrea Yates sat in a jail cell and Rusty Yates had to deal with a demanding media that not only wanted a scoop but also wanted an answer. Why would any mother murder all of her children?

The Crime Scene

The Yates home in 2011

The house today (2013)

Authorities who responded to the scene described Yates as unemotional, unkempt, and soaking wet. One officer testified that she appeared "worn out" from drowning Noah, 7, John, 5, Paul, 3, Luke, 2, and Mary, 6 months.

Confession

The Yates children ranged in age from six months to seven years, and all of them had been named after figures from the Bible: Noah, John, Luke, Paul, and Mary. Four were boys and the infant a girl.

Once they were known to be dead, the children were left in place for three hours to await the medical examiner's van. Rusty, 36, was kept outside his own home, says Suzy Spenser in *Breaking Point*, for five long hours. He told the police that his wife was ill and had been suffering from depression. She'd been on medication.

At Houston Police headquarters, an officer turned on a tape recorder to take the formal statement of the woman who had already admitted to killing all of her children. Her name was Andrea Pia Yates and she was 36 years old. She stared straight ahead as she answered questions and said, with little energy, that she understood her rights.

"Who killed your children?" the officer asked.

"I killed my children." Her eyes were blank.

"Why did you kill your children?"

"Because I'm a bad mother."

For about seventeen minutes, they pressed her for details of exactly how she had proceeded that morning.

She had gotten out of bed around 8:10 and had waited for her husband, Rusty, to leave for work at nine. The children were all awake and eating cereal. Andrea had some, too.

Once Rusty was gone, Andrea went into the bathroom to turn on the water and fill the tub. The water came within three inches from the top.

Then one by one, she drowned three of her sons, Luke, age 2; Paul, age 3; and John, age 5. She put them in facedown and held them as they struggled. As each one died, she then placed him face up on a bed, still wet, and then covered all three with a sheet. Each had struggled just a few minutes. Next was six-month-old Mary, the youngest, who had been in the bathroom all this time, sitting on the floor in her bassinet and crying. When Andrea was finished with Mary, she left her floating in the water and called to her oldest son, Noah.

He came right away. "What happened to Mary?" he asked. Then apparently realizing what his mother was doing, he ran from the bathroom but Andrea chased him down and dragged him back to the tub. She forced him in face down and drowned him right next to Mary. She admitted in her confession that he had put up the biggest struggle of all. At times he managed to slip from her grasp and get some air, but she always managed to push him back down. His last words were, "I'm sorry." She left him there floating in a tub full of feces, urine and vomit, where police found him. She lifted Mary out and placed her on the bed with her other brothers. Andrea gently covered her before calling the police and her husband. It was time.

Had the children done something to make her want to kill them? The officer asked.

No.

You weren't mad?

No.

She admitted that she was taking medication for depression and she named her doctor, whom she had seen two days earlier. She believed she was not a good mother because the children were "not developing correctly." She'd been having thoughts about hurting them over the past two years. She needed to be punished for not being a good mother.

The questioning officer was confused. How was the murder of her children a way to achieve that? "Did you want the criminal justice system to punish you?" he asked.

"Yes."

She had almost done the same thing two months earlier, she admitted. She had filled the tub. Rusty was home at the time, so she just didn't do it.

The officer asked for the birth dates of each of her children and then stopped the tape.

The media soon learned that Andrea had suffered from depression for at least two years and had been hospitalized for attempted suicide.

By the end of that first awful day, Andrea Yates was charged with capital murder for "intentionally and knowingly" causing the deaths of three of her children, using water as a weapon. She was not charged in the deaths of the two youngest boys. There was no indication on this report, says Spencer that she suffered from mental illness.

Andrea Yates in Jail

Yet Rusty was telling the media that she had suffered bouts of serious depression since the birth of their fourth child two years earlier.

In fact, her most recent psychiatrist, Dr. Mohammed Saeed, had called Rusty on the day of the drownings. He appeared to be stunned and apparently wanted to make it clear that he had believed that Rusty's mother was always at the home.

On the local radio, talk show hosts were buzzing, asking people to call in and express their outrage at a mother who would do such a thing. They tried her in the court of public opinion and found her worthy of death.

However, Rusty had made a decision. He felt torn, he said, but it was not his wife who had killed the children, but her illness. He went out to the throng of reporters and, holding a portrait of the once-happy family, told them everything he could recall from that dreadful day. He believed that the Andrea he knew was not the one who had turned against their kids. As he searched desperately for reasons that hadn't been obvious before, he made it clear that he intended to support her.

"She wasn't in the right frame of mind," he said.

Five small caskets

And tears from a grieving father

Russell Yates, center right, follows behind the casket of his oldest child, Noah, as the caskets of the other four children wait to be loaded into hearses after a funeral service yesterday in Clear Lake, a suburb of Houston.

The father of five children said goodbye to them in a hushed church service, weeping as he reached into their five white caskets to tuck a blanket beside each body.

"I'm sorry I didn't get to see you grow up," Russell Yates told Mary, at 6 months the youngest of his lost children.

The caskets were arrayed in an arc, each with a ribbon bearing a child's name. After a 75-minute service, the caskets were wheeled slowly from the church and taken to a nearby cemetery, where Yates cried as he touched each one.

"I can't possibly tell you everything there is to know about each one of them," Russell Yates told some 300 mourners at the Clear Lake Church of Christ, a few blocks from the

Yates home. "But I can give you a glimpse of who they were."

Six-month-old Mary was dressed in a pink sleeper. Her 3-year-old brother Paul was to her left and 2-year-old Luke to her right. Noah, 7, wore a multicolored sweater emblazoned with a truck. John, 5, wore an orange and black sweater.

Noah, Yates said, was intelligent, independent and a lover of bugs; John, rough and tumble with a great smile; Paul the most well-behaved; Luke was the troublemaker, the one most likely to challenge boundaries; and Mary was the "princess" of the family.

"If the Lord giveth and the Lord taketh away, that's exactly what he's done," Yates said. "He gave me all these children and now he's taken them away."

The white caskets were arrayed in an arc, each with a ribbon bearing a child's name. After a service of about 75 minutes, the caskets were wheeled slowly from the church and taken to a nearby cemetery, where Yates wept as he touched each one.

Evaluation

On June 22, Andrea appeared before Judge Belinda Hill and listened to prosecutor Kaylynn Williford state the case against her. It was Williford's first capital case and she went at it with all she had. Andrea then quietly said that she did not have an attorney. The judge appointed public defender Bob Scott, who requested a gag order. The county prosecutor's office had not yet said whether they would seek the death penalty, but Williford and her partner, Joseph Owmby, told the press that they did not intend to make their decisions public. Owmby said that it was the most horrendous case he'd ever seen.

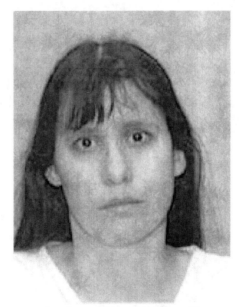

Andrea Yates prison ID

Rusty looked for an attorney to take Andrea's case. He talked with family friend, George Parnham, who agreed to get involved. His first act was to get family members in to see Andrea. Spencer describes the initial meeting between Rusty and Andrea, according to Rusty. Andrea's first words were, "You will be greatly rewarded." She rejected the attorney and told Rusty to "Have a nice life." He was completely confused. Later he found out that she had been given a sedative.

Wendell Odom came on the case to assist Parnham, and he said that all Andrea asked when he sat with her was what kind of plea they were going to enter and insisted she did not want to plead not guilty. He watched her, with her sunken eyes and hair hanging over her face, and believed she might not even be competent to stand trial. She had said that she heard the voice of Satan coming out of the walls of her cell. Dr. Lucy Puryear, a psychiatrist from the Baylor College of Medicine, said on Court TV's *Mugshots* program "She was the sickest person I had ever seen in my life." In those early days, Andrea was unbathed, dressed in an orange prison uniform, and seemingly unaware of what was going on around her.

She was shaking, and every now and then she absently scratched at her head. Puryear believed she was suffering from postpartum psychosis.

Andrea's medical records were subpoenaed from the Devereux Texas Treatment Network, where she'd last been seen.

While postpartum depression occurs in up to twenty percent of women who have children, psychotic manifestations are much rarer, and thus much less understood. Only one in five hundred births result in the mother's postpartum psychosis, says forensic psychiatrist Michael Welner. Unlike in Britain, where the mental health system watches mothers for months afterward for signs of depression and mood swings, people in America have a difficult time understanding how hormonal shifts can actually cause violent hallucinations and thoughts. Such women can become incoherent, paranoid, irrational, and delusional. They may have outright hallucinations, and are at risk of committing suicide or harming their child—particularly "for the child's own good." The woman herself will not recognize it as an illness, so those countries that have programs for it generally advise immediate hospitalization.

A psychiatric examination was ordered for Andrea. One psychiatrist, featured on *Mugshots*, asked Andrea what she thought would happen to the children. She indicated that she believed God would "take them up." He reversed the question and asked what might have happened if she had not taken their lives.

"I guess they would have continued stumbling," which meant "they would have gone to hell."

He wanted to know specifically what they had done to give her the idea they weren't behaving properly. She responded that they didn't treat Rusty's mother well, adding that, "They didn't do things God likes."

Five days later, on the day of the children's funeral, the judge issued a gag order, effectively ending information leaking to the press. For the time being, anyway. Items kept leaking out.

Russell Yates

Time reporter Michelle McCalope attended the June 27
funeral for the five children at Clear Lake Church of Christ
and published an account of the service. Rusty looked tired
and grim in the unbearable humidity. He looked at the
small cream-colored caskets, open for viewing, and placed
Mary's favorite blanket inside hers. The baby was dressed
in pink. Rusty cried as he spoke his final words to her. He
did the same at each of the other four open coffins, telling
them they were now in good hands and placing some
favorite item inside.

He gave a half-hour eulogy that addressed each child's
personality and offered family stories. He had a projector
on which he showed pictures of the children, happy and
having fun. Then he offered some scriptures, saying that
what had happened was God's will. At the end, he sat
down, clearly still in shock.

Andrea's relatives attended as well.

By June 28, a staff writer for ABC News predicted what might happen to Yates. While juries tend to punish the killing of strangers harshly, they often are more lenient with mothers. Juries have a difficult time in America sending a mother to lethal gas or the electric chair. In 2000, Christina Riggs was a notable exception. She killed her two children in a suicide attempt, and was put to death in Arkansas. At the time of the article, there were eight other women on death row, yet approximately 180 children are murdered annually by their mothers.

Typically, a woman has a believably tragic story to go along with her deed, although some like Mary Beth Tinning, Susan Smith, and Marie Noe turned out to have killed for reasons other than their initial excuses. Thus, excuses become suspicious. And sometimes an act is so overwhelming that no mental condition seems to count as a reasonable explanation.

In Loving Memory
Of Five Little Angels
Who Left Too Soon

The Yates Children

Legal Decisions

On July 31, a Houston grand jury indicted Andrea Yates for capital murder in the cases of Noah, John, and Mary. Because she had killed someone under the age of six and had killed more than one person, she was eligible for the death penalty. There was talk that the prosecutors would keep the other two deaths as fallback, in case they did not get convictions. Judge Hill ordered a third psychiatric examination, with the results due before Yates' arraignment.

A deteriorating Andrea went to court on August 8 to enter an insanity defense. She was even thinner now than she had been in June, although she had been medicated with Haldol, the only drug that had worked for her. A rudimentary psychological report done for the court indicated that she was competent to stand trial. But Parnham and Odom weren't content. They wanted a jury to make that determination, since their own psychiatrists had concluded that she was not competent. In other words, she was not able to participate in her own defense with a reasonable degree of rational understanding and comprehension of the court proceedings.

Defense attorney George Parnham

The judge granted their request to look at the medical testimony that Dr. Saeed's gave to the grand jury and set a date for a competency hearing. She granted the prosecution's request to have their own experts examine Andrea.

The next day, the prosecutors stated that they would be seeking the death penalty. No one was allowed to comment publicly, not even Rusty. Yet on September 5, he met with Ed Bradley from *60 Minutes* to answer questions. He turned over videos of the children and talked about Andrea, but shied away from his feelings about the forthcoming trial. He was also prepared to answer questions for *Time* magazine and anticipated that they would come out after the hearing. He had hired an attorney, Edward Mallett, to fight the gag order. At some point during the hearing, DA Chuck Rosenthal spoke with the *60 Minutes* crew as well.

On September 18 (postponed one week due to the September 11 terrorist attacks on the U.S.), a jury selection began for the competency proceeding. Eleven women and one man were selected. In *Breaking Point*, Spencer gives a comprehensive account of the proceedings.

Andrea's attorneys filed hundreds of pages of documentation on her history of mental illness. Their experts claimed she was not ready, while the prosecution experts were about to declare her competent. Andrea's mother and siblings were subpoenaed, as were several jail employees. The lawyers argued over the State's psychologist seeing Andrea without the defense's knowledge, and the judge made a ruling that the information could not be used—although toward the end of the hearing, it was.

Parnham called Dr. Gerald Harris, a clinical psychologist who had interviewed Andrea in prison on four occasions. On June 25, she had shown signs of psychosis and hallucinations. She said she had seen Satan in her cell and he was talking to her. She had a difficult time processing Harris's questions and sometimes did not seem to hear them at all. She did make it clear that she wanted to be executed so that she and Satan, who possessed her, would be destroyed. She had insisted that she would not enter a plea of not guilty. She did not need an attorney, and she wanted her hair cut into the shape of a crown. She believed the number of the Antichrist, 666, was imprinted on her scalp.

By the end of August, on medication, she was much improved. She reported no hallucinations and was able to hold a conversation. She still had delusions about Satan but insisted she was not mentally ill. Her intelligence was above average, but she had difficulty remembering things—an important issue for competency. She believed that Satan lived inside her and the way to be rid of him was for her to be killed.

Andrea Yates in court

Dr Lauren Marangell, an expert on depression, testified about changes in the brain during different psychological states. She also provided a map of Andrea's psychotic episodes since 1999. She concluded that Andrea would be competent in the foreseeable future, with continued treatment.

The prosecutors took their witnesses—mostly prison staff—over the thirteen points involved in assessing competency. Then they questioned Dr. Steve Rubenzer, who had spent over ten hours with the defendant and who had administered a competency examination on several successive occasions—the very assessments that were in dispute because they were done without Parnham's knowledge. It was his opinion that the defendant's comprehension had improved over time and that she did pass the state's competency stipulations. However, he believed that Andrea Yates did have a serious mental illness and he thought her psychotic features were only in partial remission.

Under cross-examination, he admitted that she believed that Satan inhabited her and that Governor Bush would destroy him. But Bush had not been the governor of Texas at that time.

Two more mental health experts testified, and while they were divided on the competency issue, all recognized psychosis in Andrea's condition and no one thought she was malingering.

On September 24, the jury deemed Andrea Pia Yates competent to stand trial. The defense quickly prepared motions.

Now it was time for both sides to learn more about who she was, what her mental health history was, the quality of her marriage, and what factors had been involved in her fateful decision.

The Evolution of an Illness

Andrea Yates was born Andrea Kennedy on July 2, 1964 into a middle class family in Houston, the youngest of five children. She had developed a very close relationship with her father, a high school teacher, and she liked to help other people. She graduated from high school as class valedictorian and had been captain of the swim team. She had been shy with boys but was goal-oriented like the rest of her family, and had good friends. She earned a nursing degree from the University of Texas Health Science Center and found work as a registered nurse. She quit after she married and had her first child.

Timothy Roche delved deep into her history for *Time* and discovered a rather disturbing picture of a troubled family, including a long history of mental illness for Yates. But there was more, emphasized in a documentary for Court TV's *Mugshots*. The form mental illness takes often has an outside influence, and this one was insidious.

Andrea and Rusty had met when they were both 25. Rusty had seen her swimming in a pool of his apartment complex and had decided he was interested in her. She introduced herself to him and they dated for three years. In 1993, they were married and a year later had Noah. They planned on having as many children as came along, whatever God wanted for them, and told friends they expected six.

Yet soon after Noah was born, Andrea began to have violent visions: she saw someone being stabbed. She thought she heard Satan speak to her. However, she and her husband had idealistic, Bible-inspired notions about family and motherhood, so she kept her tormenting secrets to herself. She didn't realize how much mental illness there was in her own family, from depression to bipolar disorder—which can contribute to postpartum psychosis. In her initial stages, she remained undiagnosed and untreated. She kept her secrets from everyone.

Rusty introduced Andrea to a preacher who had impressed him in college, a man named Michael Woroniecki. He was a sharp-witted, sharp-tongued, self-proclaimed "prophet" who preached a simple message about following Jesus but who was so belligerent in public about sinners going to hell (which included most people) that he was often in trouble. He even left Michigan, according to *Mugshots*, to avoid prosecution.

Rusty corresponded with Woroniecki, who wandered around with his family for several years in a bus, and eventually he believed he had found the Holy Spirit. Woroniecki spent a lot of time in his street sermons and letters to correspondents judging them for their sins and warning them about losing God's love. In particular, he emphasized that people were accountable for children, and woe to the person who might cause even one to stumble. He once stated, "I feel like I need a sledge hammer to get you to listen." He denounced Catholicism, the religion with which Andrea had grown up, and stressed the sinful state of her soul.

He also preached austerity, and his ideas were probably instrumental in the way the Yates's decided to live. As Andrea had one child after another, she took on the task of home-schooling them with Christian-only texts and trying to do what the Woroniecki and his wife, Rachel, told her.

"From the letters I have that Rachel Woroniecki wrote to Andrea," says Suzy Spencer on *Mugshots*, "it was, 'You are evil. You are wicked. You are a daughter of Eve, who is a wicked witch. The window of opportunity for us to minister to you is closing. You have to repent *now*.'"

According to a former follower, the religion preached by the Woronieckis involves the idea that women have Eve's witch nature and need to be subservient to men. The preacher judged harshly those mothers who were permissive and who allowed their children to go in the wrong direction. In other words, if the mother was going to Hell for some reason, so would the children.

After two more children had come along, Rusty decided to "travel light," and made his small family sell their possessions and live first in a recreational vehicle and then in a bus that Woroniecki had converted for his religious crusade and sold to them. Andrea didn't complain—she was the type of woman who just went along with decisions---but she got pregnant again and had a miscarriage. Yet it wasn't long before she recovered, was again pregnant and had her fourth child, making their 350-square-foot living quarters rather cramped. She continued to correspond with the Woronieckis and to receive their warnings. They thought it was better to kill oneself than to mislead a child in the way of Jesus—a sentiment she would repeat later in prison interviews.

Not surprisingly, she sank into a depression. She was lonely. She tried to be a good mother, but the pressures were building. At the same time, her father grew ill with Alzheimer's and she had to help care for him. Then things got bad.

Michael Woroniecki

The Bottom Falls Out

In 1999, Andrea called Rusty at work and told him she needed help. When he arrived home, he found her shaking and chewing her fingers, so he took her and the children to his parents' home, where she said she felt better. But then she tried to kill herself with a drug overdose from her father's medication, and with Andrea's mother's help, Rusty finally got her into treatment. Later she said she had just wanted to "sleep forever." She was diagnosed with a major depressive disorder. She admitted to anxiety and having overwhelming thoughts. Those who observed her and spoke to Rusty, according to several accounts, believed that he was controlling.

Andrea was prescribed Zoloft for depression, but she was resistant to taking medication, ostensibly because she wanted to be able to breast-feed her youngest child. Many presumed it was because the Woronieckis would judge her harshly for it. She soon withdrew and began to sleep a lot. She worried about the hospital bill and would not talk about her home life. The insurance money ran out.

The ailing mother was discharged and another psychiatrist switched her to Zyprexa, an antipsychotic drug for bipolar disorders and schizophrenia. Andrea flushed the pills down the toilet. Then she got worse.

She told her psychiatrist that she was hearing voices and seeing visions again about getting a knife. She began to scratch at herself, leaving sores on her legs. Then Rusty found her in the bathroom one day pressing a knife to her throat. He took it away and got her hospitalized.

Andrea confessed to one doctor that she was afraid she might hurt someone. She refused medication and withdrew from all efforts to help. She refused to answer questions. Finally, she was given a shot of the antipsychotic drug Haldol. She got a little better, and then worse, so she was given more Haldol. She improved slightly, but would not eat. She was afraid of what her visions might mean.

Relatives had pressured Rusty to buy a house for his family, so he did, moving the bus into the yard by the garage at their new Clear Lake home.

Andrea sometimes talked with social workers, but often changed her story. She'd been suicidal, she had not been suicidal. She did admit that she got anxious when stressed and she vaguely associated stress with her children. The doctor anticipated that electroshock therapy might eventually be needed. It was controversial, but had shown some positive benefits for depressed older women. Andrea, he wrote, also needed to develop coping strategies for stress. For two days, she refused her medication. Then she was discharged with more prescriptions for pills that she would avoid taking.

She continued therapy, which included group therapy, and said she wanted to get off medication so she could get pregnant again. She seemed anxious, so her outpatient therapist, Dr. Eileen Starbranch, switched her to the sedative Ativan. She worried that Andrea's plan for more children could result in psychosis. Andrea did not take the Ativan.

At home, Andrea remained secretive and seemingly obsessed with reading the Bible. Rusty thought that was a positive thing. Andrea's therapist took her off Haldol, but had her continue with several other antidepressants. Andrea decided to discontinue them on her own. Despite doctor's warnings to have no more children, they had a baby girl, Mary, late in 2000. Rusty believed he would spot the onset of depression and get help if needed. He was sure any bad effects could be controlled with medication.

To this point, she'd experienced several episodes of psychotic hallucinations, survived two suicide attempts, taken a number of different medications, and been diagnosed in several institutions with major depression. Now she had five young children to care for, three of whom were still in diapers.

When Andrea's father died a few months later, she stopped functioning. She wouldn't feed the baby, she became malnourished herself, and she drifted into a private world. Rusty forced her back into treatment at Devereux Texas Treatment Network in April under yet another doctor, Ellen Albritton, who put her on antidepressants.

Then psychiatrist Mohammed Saeed took over her care. He received scanty medical records from her previous treatment and no information from her, so he put Andrea on Risperdol, a new drug, rather than Haldol. He had not heard about hallucinations, and he observed no psychosis himself, so he felt Haldol was unnecessary. However, Suzy Spencer indicates that the notes kept on Andrea were disorganized and scribbled over someone else's chart. The descriptions of Andrea's condition, which was near catatonia, were vague. Saeed discharged Andrea into her husband's care, with a suggestion for partial hospitalization, and gave her a two-week prescription.

Rusty's mother came from Tennessee to help out with the children, but Andrea wound up back in the hospital. When she started to eat and shower, she was sent home, with the provision that she continues outpatient therapy. One day she filled the tub and her mother-in-law asked why. She responded, "In case I need it."

It seemed a strange statement, and no one knew how to interpret it, so they let it pass. They did not see the forewarning except in hindsight.

Yet Rusty was worried, so he took Andrea back to the doctor, telling him that she was not doing well. According to Roche, Saeed reportedly assured him that Andrea did not need shock treatment or Haldol, but Spencer says that he did suggest shock treatments and did prescribe Haldol. Andrea was shuffled back and forth, and early in June, Dr. Saeed took her off the antipsychotic medication.

Then on June 18, Rusty was back. Andrea was having problems. Saeed supposedly told Andrea to "think positive thoughts," and to see a psychologist for therapy. However, he says that he did warn Rusty that she should not be left alone. Rusty told author Suzy Spencer that on that day Saeed had cut Andrea's medication—now it was Effexor-- too drastically and he had protested, but the doctor had reassured him it was "fine."

Rusty had filled the prescription, still confused as to why the doctor thought that an obviously sick woman was doing okay. That was two days before the fatal incident.

Andrea sat at home during those days in a near-catatonic state, and to Rusty she seemed nervous. However, he did not think that she was a danger to the children, so on June 20 he left her alone. Since his mother was coming, he felt sure everything would be fine. Andrea was eating cereal out of a box, which was uncharacteristic of her, but her demeanor seemed okay. He didn't think a few minutes alone would be a problem.

How wrong he was.

On that morning, she had a plan.

Legal Maneuvers

On October 30, Parnham and Odom filed nearly three-dozen pre-trial motions, including a rather crucial request that the Court reconsider a procedure in the Texas Criminal Code that prohibited jurors from learning that a verdict of not guilty by reason of insanity (NGRI) was not an outright acquittal. It involved sending the person to a mental institution for treatment and periodic re-evaluation. Those defendants did not just walk free. The attorneys believed that such knowledge could play a strong role in how the jury made a decision in this case.

The two attorneys also wanted Yates's confession thrown out because she had not been competent to waive her rights and they asked the Court to declare the insanity plea, as it was stated in Texas law, to be unconstitutional, because it was not in touch with what we now know about the true nature of mental illness.

In November, the prosecution's psychiatrist, Dr. Park Dietz, came to interview Andrea. A nationally prominent psychiatrist who consulted for the FBI and worked on such cases as serial killer Jeffrey Dahmer and Susan Smith (who also drowned her children), he generally only worked for the prosecution. He had limited knowledge of postpartum depression.

Dr. Park Dietz testifies in court

The interview was taped, and after the trial it was released
to the public. Andrea told Dietz that at the time of the
killings in June, Satan was inside her, giving her
directions. "I was pretty determined," she admitted, "to do
what Satan told me to do." She also indicated that she felt
that by killing her children before they went downhill
morally, she was ensuring they would get into heaven.
That's the only place where they would be safe.

Dietz asked her several times whether she knew that what
she had done was wrong and she answered yes. She had
planned for at least a month to kill them at some point
when she was alone with them.

December was a difficult month. Andrea's lawyers tried to fight the capital murder charge, and failed. While they were granted a number of motions, they did not get those they felt were most crucial. In particular, the jury would not learn that in the event of an NGRI verdict, Andrea would go into treatment.

Both Rusty and the police officers who had gone to the scene testified at a hearing. The judge ruled that Andrea's 911 call and her confession would be admissible. Rusty had spoken out in September, violating the gag order, and his *60 Minutes* interview was broadcast on December 9. A special independent prosecutor was appointed to probe the violation by both Rusty and DA Rosenthal, but the talk was that he would delay it until after the trial, which was fast approaching. By the end of the trial, the issue would be moot.

Jury selection began on January 7, 2002. It took a week, and in the end, eight women and four men were seated. Seven had children and two had degrees in psychology. They were "death qualified." The trial date was set for February.

Andrea would have to prove that on the morning when she had drowned her children she'd had a mental disease or defect that prohibited her from understanding that what she had done was wrong. Since she was claiming that she did indeed know that it was wrong, the attorneys needed experts who could prove that her manner of processing this information was in itself rooted in psychosis. Not only did they have to meet one of the most restrictive standards in the country for insanity, they had to educate the jury in ideas about mental illness that were rife among the public with stereotypes and misperception and to help them get beyond the literal interpretation of "right" and "wrong." A mock trial that the defense had tried had already shown them that a jury in their area might have a difficult time accepting that someone can confess to such a crime and not understand what she had done.

They had to present a very strong case.

The Case Against Her

Andrea Yates was being tried on two counts of capital murder—one for the two older boys and one for Mary. Because it had caught the nation's attention and because it was so controversial, her case was to become a high-profile arena for the battle of medical experts.

Opening statements began on February 18. The prosecution claimed that Andrea Yates had drowned her five children and had known it was illegal and wrong. There would be plenty of signs supporting that. For example, she waited until her husband had gone to work so he would not stop her, she prepared for it, she was methodical, and she called the police afterward. Owmby and Williford wanted to keep the jury focused on whether she knew right from wrong at the time of the offense. Her mental illness, they would insist, was not relevant to that.

Prosecutor Joseph Owmby

The defense said that she did not know what she was doing because she had been legally insane. She'd been suffering from postpartum depression with psychotic features and her delusions had driven her to kill her children. Her illness, said Parnham, "was so severe, so longstanding that Andrea Yates' ability to think in abstract terms, to give narrative responses, to be able to connect the dots was impaired." He explained that it was important that they not give the impression to the jury that they were claiming a "devil made me do it" defense. They were trying to indicate the disordered nature of Andrea's thinking.

In other words, the primary question in this case was whether Yates had killed the children while in a state of disabling psychosis or had knowingly done it to escape a life she hated or to punish her husband.

The real problem for the defense was that medication had stabilized Andrea over the eight months since the crimes had occurred and in court she appeared to be normal---a far cry from her initial prison interview on the day of the crime. Yet they ethically could not have withheld medication for demonstration purposes. It was a dilemma.

The prosecution laid out its case first, with the 911 call, the testimony of police officers who responded to the scene, Andrea's prison confession, and with autopsy reports from medical examiners. Jurors heard about how one child had strands of his mother's hair clamped in his little fist. They showed photos and home videos of the children, while Andrea cried.

Andrea's mother-in-law then took the stand and discussed her observations of "her precious daughter-in-law" during the time she had been helping with the children. Mrs. Yates described Andrea as nearly catatonic, staring into space, and did not think she was aware of what she was doing when she killed the children. She was a better witness for the defense, it seemed.

The prosecutors entered the children's pajamas into evidence, over Parnham's insistent protest; to "show" how much smaller these children were than their mother. Parnham believed it was merely to inflame the jury, but Judge Hill sided with Owmby. He then worked hard at proving beyond a reasonable doubt that Andrea Yates had knowingly murdered her children.

After three days, the prosecution rested and the defense called its first witness.

Andrea's Defense

During the defense's presentation of proof of Andrea's insanity, Parnham and Odom used prison psychiatrist Melissa Ferguson to testify to Andrea's state of mind soon after her arrest. After being placed on medications that allowed her to process questions and to talk, she admitted to her fears about Satan: He had spoken to her and the children through cartoons they were watching on television. They were bad because they were eating too much candy. He demanded that she kill the children, and to be rid of him, she believed she had to get the death penalty. Her children, she said, could never be saved, because she had not raised them right. She had decided on drowning because stabbing was too bloody.

Rusty also took the stand and described his wife's manner with the children. He admitted that he had not grasped the full extent of his wife's illness and often just did not know what to do. Andrea did not tell him about the hallucinations or voices and he had assumed that the doctors he took her to had done whatever could be done. He admitted being frustrated with Dr. Saeed's refusal to use Haldol or keep her hospitalized.

Saeed had written in her records that she had no symptoms of psychosis. He went on the stand during the start of the third week of trial. He had diagnosed her with depression with psychotic features but did not have evidence that she was psychotic two days before the fatal incident. Parnham accused him of doctoring his notes to protect himself, based on his perception that the handwriting about the lack of psychotic features was smaller than other writing on the report. Saeed vehemently stated that he had written the notes on the same day.

Then Andrea's mother took the stand to talk for ten minutes about Andrea being a wonderful mother. There was no cross-examination.

Now it was time for the big guns. Odom and Parnham called on psychiatrists Phillip Resnick from Case Western University in Ohio, Steve Rosenblatt, and Lucy Puryear to explain that Andrea suffered from schizophrenic delusions and had believed that killing her children was the right thing to do.

The defense psychiatrists tried hard to show the jury that Andrea was incapable of knowing what she had done within a normal context of interpretation.

"It's not like she could come up with a list of options," Puryear said. "She was psychotic at the time and driven by delusions that [the children] were going to Hell and she must save them."

Rosenblatt, who interviewed her five days after the killings said that he observed that she was in a deep state of psychosis, and it would have taken her weeks to get that sick. He concluded that she had been in that hallucinatory state at the time of the incident. He could not say why she had stopped taking her medication.

They described Andrea's suicide attempts and her hallucinations after her first child was born. Puryear talked about her shame over such ideations and her need for secrecy.

She also educated the jury in the difference between postpartum depression and postpartum psychosis, and indicated that Andrea was suspicious that Satan may have influenced her doctors.

Dr. Phillip Resnick

Dr. Resnick, a specialist in parents who kill their children, described the killings as "altruistic." He admitted that Andrea did know that what she was doing was illegal but believed her decision to kill her children was nevertheless right, for the protection of their eternal souls. He believed, after seeing her in her cell on two different occasions that she suffered from schizophrenia and depression. While he contradicted the other doctors, he said each had his own interpretation of the data.

Rebuttal

Dr. Park Dietz, in from TAG, his threat assessment firm in California, was a rebuttal witness after the defense presented its case. Much was made in the media about the fact the Resnick and Dietz were once again head to head. They had been on opposite sides of several other high-profile cases and Dietz usually won the day. His forte was to make complicated psychological issues simple for juries, and in the Yates case he used a Power Point presentation to do so. While he admitted that Andrea was seriously ill, possibly even schizophrenic, he also insisted that she had nevertheless known that what she was doing was wrong.

He pointed out that she had not acted like a mother who believed she was saving her children from Satan, and she had kept her long-festering plan a secret from others. Thus, while she knew she was having delusions about harming others, she had done nothing to protect them. She even admitted she knew that what she had done was wrong—it was a sin---and by Texas law, these facts were sufficient for the jury to convict Yates of first-degree murder. She knew she deserved the death penalty and that it was a punishment for doing something wrong. She also believed that God would judge her act as bad, and Dietz interpreted her covering of the bodies with a sheet as evidence of guilt. The fact that she had not comforted and reassured them in death indicated that she had not killed them as an act of love and protection.

"Ordinarily when someone keeps a criminal plan secret," Dietz said, "they do it because it's wrong."

He tended to blame others, notably Rusty. He described the note from Dr. Saeed in her medical records that she was not to be left alone. That implied that she was severely impaired and was not safe to leave with children. He pointed out that she did not follow the advice of her various doctors and made decisions based on her belief that she knew what was best for herself. She had been living in unhealthy conditions during her illness and not gotten good continuous care. In her cell when Dietz interviewed her, Andrea had admitted that it had been a bad decision to kill the children, and said, "I shouldn't have done it." She thought the devil had left after she committed the crime. "He destroys and then leaves."

To counter much of what the defense's psychiatrists had laid out, Dietz opened up possibilities to the jury when he said that Andrea's psychosis may have worsened the day following the incident, while in jail where psychiatrists first saw her. "There seemed to be new delusions and disorganized thinking on June 21." The motive for killing her children, he indicated, appeared to be the same as her suicide: to escape an intolerable, high-stress situation.

Dietz also had learned that Andrea was an avid viewer of the television show, *Law and Order*, for which he consulted, and he believed that an episode of that show in which a mother drowns her child in a bathtub had inspired Andrea. His observation gave her actions the quality of premeditation.

Dietz was the final act before both sides summed up their cases for the jury.

Rusty Yates, seen here praying, supported his wife's
defense while struggling with the loss
of his children. Rusty became a vocal opponent of the death
penalty.

Verdict

For closing statements, Kaylynn Williford asked the jury to be silent for three minutes so they could experience the amount of time each child had endured the drowning process before dying. It was a dramatic maneuver and Parnham could do nothing to prevent it. He wrapped up his case by emphasizing the points the psychiatrists had made. It was clear that he cared very much what might happen to the woman in his charge.

The trial had lasted three weeks, but it took the jury less than three hours on March 12, 2002, to return a verdict of guilty. Rusty buried his face in his hands and moaned. Andrea looked back at her brother Brian and tried to smile, but instead she began to cry and turned away to walk off with the prison guard.

"The way the case unfolded," said Owmby. "I was confident that the jury would find her guilty and reject the insanity defense." Williford, said, "I think the jury focused on the children."

The nation now debated whether Andrea Yates should be sentenced to death. Many felt the verdict was unfair and hoped the jury would do what they considered the right thing and at least give her only life in prison. Many others felt that a jury that had been quick to find her guilty might show no such compassion. Some raised the issue that the jury might have made a different decision had they understood that an NGRI verdict would have kept Andrea institutionalized and would have ensured mental health treatment. Why weren't they allowed to have that information?

Then the defense attorneys, says Roche, discovered a significant flaw in Park Dietz's testimony. The television episode that he claimed had inspired Andrea and which prosecutors had used to show premeditation had never aired. Dietz sent a letter admitting to his error and to the fact that Andrea had never mentioned the show to him.

He also did post-trial interviews in which he said that he disagreed with the way the state of Texas worded the insanity plea. He believed that people as sick as Andrea Yates should be handled differently than other criminals were.

In light of all this, Parnham and Odom asked for a mistrial. Judge Hill said no.

During the penalty phase that spring, the same jury quickly returned a sentence of life in prison (in less than forty minutes) rather than death, and Andrea Yates received this news with little emotion. She would be eligible for parole in 2041, when she was 77. She was sent to Mountain View Unit, a state psychiatric prison in eastern Texas.

Rusty announced that his family had been mishandled by the mental health system. He did not see that he had been adequately warned and he insisted that Andrea had not been adequately treated. He decided to set up a Web site to inform people about mental illness and to post pictures and facts about his children.

Postpartum Psychosis:

A Tough Sell

On October 21, 2002 in Kansas City, Mary Bass, 32, was
convicted of two counts of second-degree murder in the
deaths of her two male children. She claimed that another
personality named "Sharon" that she could not control had
abused them to the point of death. She had locked them in
a room and starved them, burning their legs and feet in
scalding water to punish them. Psychologists said that she
suffered from depression, posttraumatic stress syndrome,
schizophrenia, and multiple personality disorder. She was
also suicidal. She told police, "I killed my baby. I should
go to jail." Social workers had seen the abuse but did
nothing to remove the children.

In Wisconsin, Kristin Scott, 22, pleaded not guilty by
reason of mental deficiency on July 18, 2003, to charges
that in January she let her newborn infant daughter die and
hid the remains in a plastic tub. She had also similarly
hidden the remains of a child she claimed had been
stillborn in April 2001. Scott's parents discovered the
remains of the most recent baby when Scott moved to
Texas in June, leaving the tub behind in their home. She
said that she had secretly given birth in January and
because she was afraid of what people would say, the baby
had to die. If convicted of reckless homicide and hiding a
corpse, she faces seventy-five years in prison.

Naomi Gaines, mugshot

Naomi Gaines, 24, had suffered for a long   history of postpartum depression and mania. On July 6, 2003, she took her fourteen-month-old twins, Supreme Knowledge Allah and Sincere Understanding Allah, to the Mississippi River near St. Paul and dropped them both from a bridge 75 feet over the water. Then she jumped in after them, yelling "Freedom!" She and one boy survived when rescued in time, but the other infant drowned and his body was recovered several miles downriver near an island. She is charged with second-degree murder.

Also in Minnesota, Khoua Her, 24, strangled her six children, ages 5 to 11, because she was depressed over her responsibilities. The police had been to her home fifteen times in a year and a half, responding to domestic violence calls, but social workers had not noticed any apparent danger to the children. The mother, who called 911 after the slaughter and spoke of suicide, was transported to the hospital with an extension cord still loosely tied around her neck. The children were found throughout the house. In a plea deal, she received a sentence of fifty years in prison.

Evonne Rodriguez killed her 4-month-old baby in 1997 in Houston, Texas, because she believed he was possessed by demons.   She had tried to "pull them out," her mother claimed, but ended up killing the child. Evonne insisted that she had heard screeching voices, "just like Hell," so she beat at her child with her hand and then choked him with a rosary. She wrapped him in plastic and threw him into water, but she concocted a story for police that he had been kidnapped—an indication that she knew what she had done was wrong. Her defense was that she was distraught over a bad relationship with her son's father that had created a state of temporary insanity. Her mother testified that she had suffered from bouts of depression. The jury acquitted her and she was sent for treatment.

In America, there are no clear standards in court for dealing with mentally ill mothers—not even in the same city.   Andrea Yates killed five children to save them from hell and got life in prison. Evonne Rodriguez killed one because of demons and was acquitted. Andrea probably had a better case; Evonne got the better deal.

On a CNN broadcast, David Williams addressed the issue of   how difficult it is to get juries to understand the kind of depression that can follow giving birth. The primary reason juries may not understand is because   such depression is temporary and treatable. Such sufferers may have been psychotic and deeply disturbed during a violent episode sometime after the birth, but by the time they go to trial, they've usually been restored to better mental health. That makes it difficult for juries who see them in their improved condition to believe these mothers were really suffering that badly.

It's also difficult in a country that views motherhood as sacred and asks women to see birth as cause for celebration to admit to postpartum depression. There's little compassion to be found for the 10 to 20 percent of mothers who really do suffer.

Twenty-nine other countries recognize postpartum depression as a legal defense, writes Williams, including Canada, Britain, and Australia. If a woman who has murdered a child under a certain age---usually one year--- can prove that her mental processes were disturbed, the maximum charge is manslaughter. They receive probation and counseling. They do not have to prove they were insane at the time of the crime.

Yet clearly   some women kill their infants for other reasons and might exploit this defense. American emphasis on free choice and personal responsibility makes it likely that juries will continue to give mental illness issues uneven recognition.

Aftermath

Andrea went to prison, but many people believed that she was not the only one who was culpable in this tragedy. Rusty had been warned not to leave her alone with the children and a doctor had taken her off medication while apparently believing that she could be a danger to herself or others. Many people believed that they shared in the blame.

Andrea Yates, mug shot

About a week after the Yates cases concluded, Harris County DA Chuck Rosenthal looked into the issue. Numerous emails had come into his office insisting that Rusty be investigated, and it did seem important to try to understand why Rusty had disregarded the doctor's instructions. He had said repeatedly that since it would be only a short time between his departure that day and his mother's arrival, he had believed his wife would be fine alone with the children. His attorney, Edward Mallett, insisted that Rusty was innocent of any wrongdoing.

"It's a tragedy that Rusty now has to defend himself after standing by his wife," Mallett said to the press.

It was Rusty's contention that those who were most responsible are the doctors and hospitals that did not treat Andrea properly, and he talked about a lawsuit against them.

In the end, there was no investigation.

Insanity Issues

The film *A Beautiful Mind* details the peculiar twist of mental illness in the case of John Nash, a brilliant economist who suffered from paranoid schizophrenia much of his life. It revealed that a person can appear to function normally to everyone around him even while trapped in delusions where imaginary people play roles and hold conversations with him. Yet his illness finally became apparent, though it took much longer to be so for him. To his mind, this was the real world.

Doctors testifying for Yates made that claim. "She did what she thought was right in the world she perceived through her psychotic eyes at the time," said psychiatrist Phillip Resnick. In other words, even if she seemed to understand the difference between right and wrong, she did not know what she was doing.

The prosecutors claimed she knew her actions were wrong,.

How these two sides lined up on different poles of interpretation illustrates the great divide between the concepts of mental illness and legal insanity in the U.S. This case made it clear that it's time for courts to better address the gap.

Yates' defense team proved her history of delusional depression, use of anti-psychotic drugs, and suicide attempts, and there's documentation that postpartum mood swings can sometimes evoke psychosis. Yet no matter how many doctors testified to Yates' mental decline, the legal issue hinged on only her mental state at the time of the offense. As Yates drowned her children one by one, even chasing down seven-year-old Noah to drag him to the tub, did she really have any awareness that what she was doing was wrong? If so, then awareness implies the ability to choose.

Past juries have been convinced that even the delusional can see the moral implication of their behavior.   Jeffrey Dahmer, the Wisconsin man who in 1991 confessed to killing 17 men, is one case in point. He admitted he'd drilled holes into the heads of some of his victims to create living zombies. He'd also envisioned building a shrine from their skulls.

Yet Dr. Park Dietz pointed out Dahmer's rational acts: When confronted by the police with one of his intended victims, he invented a misleading story and then took the young man home to kill him.   He was mentally ill, yes, but he also knew that what he was doing would land him in prison and he obviously exercised some control. Thus, he was legally sane.

Andrea Yates knew that, too.   In fact, she believed that the state's punishment for what she had done would finally defeat Satan. She fully expected to be jailed and even to be executed. Her case is similar to that of Andrew Goldstein, who in 1998 pushed Kendra Webdale in front of a Manhattan subway train, killing her instantly.

 He then leaned against a wall and said, "It was her turn." Like Yates, he'd felt compelled and also like Yates, he had stopped taking medication prescribed to alleviate the symptoms of schizophrenia. Despite seeing evidence of his psychosis in a video-taped confession, the jury convicted him of second-degree murder.

This gap between legal insanity and our evolving knowledge about mental illness has roots in a court decision in 1843. In England, Daniel M'Naghten felt persecuted by imaginary spies so he shot the Prime Minister's secretary. He did intend to kill, but his cognitive impairment was such that the court used his case to formulate a test of insanity: the defendant must not know the nature of his act or understand that it's wrong.

American courts eventually   adopted this standard. Despite reforms, the court's confidence in free will yields little room for behavior driven by distorted perceptions. In Texas, Yates was presumed sane unless her team could show that she did not know that what she did was wrong. This is partly due to the shift in their standards in 1983, after John Hinckley's assassination attempt on President Reagan ended up in NGRI. Public outrage prompted many states, including Texas, rethink NGRI. They enacted the more restrictive terms of mere knowledge of right and wrong. If you know, then you aren't insane. That's that.

Andrea Yates waited that morning for her husband to leave, knew murder was a sin, expected to be punished, and called 911, so it appears that she could control her behavior. Yet that argument depends on a simplistic idea about the relationship between awareness and choice. It may be time to legally recognize that even someone who knows the law can still be seriously impaired regarding how they conform to that law.

Mental Health Weekly published an article   that the Yates case has made lawmakers and mental health officials in Texas take another look at the issues, in particular with regard to more funding for the state's mental health system. State representative Garnet Coleman, a mental health advocate, indicated that he intended to introduce legislation to revise and refine the insanity defense laws. Legislators will be considering whether to return to a former Texas standard of acknowledging a person's inability to conform their behavior to what they know about right and wrong. It will be interesting to see what results.

An Honest Mistake?

On January 6, 2005, nearly three years after jurors sentenced Andrea Yates to life in prison, an appeals court overturned the conviction and ordered a new trial. While Yates' attorneys had appealed on nineteen separate legal grounds, including the claim that the Texas insanity standard is unconstitutional, the item that got the court's attention involved the testimony of Dr. Park Dietz, a prosecution psychiatrist. He apparently made a false statement, which figured into the way the case was presented to the jury. Who was actually to blame for this testimony is still a bit of a mystery, but the end result is that the three-judge panel of the First Appeals Court in Houston decided that the erroneous statements may have precipitated a miscarriage of justice.

Dr. Park Dietz

Essentially, it appears that the prosecution was attempting to show that Andrea Yates had seen an episode of the popular crime show, *Law and Order*, in which a woman had drowned her children, and this had given her the idea that she could kill her own children and feign mental illness. That character had supposedly been found not guilty by reason of insanity, and the episode was said to have aired not long before Yates drowned her children. Evidence was offered that Yates was a regular viewer and it was surmised that she may have seen the story and related it to her own situation: She was a beleaguered mother seeking a way out. And that's how the prosecution presented it.

But no such episode ever aired. Yates never saw a woman kill her children and thus could not have devised a copy-cat killing with a plan to fake an illness. (In fact, her years of coping with mental illness were well-documented and attested to by numerous mental health experts.) So the case presented by the prosecution was based on an idea with no factual basis. With a defendant's very life at stake, how did it happen? The stories are mixed.

KWTX.com indicated that after the appeals court decision, when Dietz was asked about his testimony, he called it an "honest mistake." He apparently indicated, according to this report, that he got the information about the episode from a conversation with the prosecution.

Yet in the same article, Yates prosecutor Joe Owmby said that he asked Dietz whether the show had ever dealt with such a case and then dropped the subject until Yates' attorneys asked about it later. He did not believe that his request had caused the false testimony. Still, the story grew.

According to the *Houston Chronicle*, before the trial a local woman had sent the Harris County district attorney's office an e-mail indicating that reruns of a show called *L. A. Law* had featured an episode with this plot. It seems that the prosecution team might have confused the two shows while discussing the case with Dietz, but a writer attending the trial who heard Dietz's statement called the producers of *Law and Order* and told defense attorney George Parnham that Dietz was in error. Dietz said that he, too, attempted to correct the error by consulting with producers. He stated that he immediately researched the matter and sent an e-mail to the prosecutors, offering to return at his own expense. The letter was dated March 14, 2002, indicating that Dietz had confused an episode based on Susan Smith and an episode inspired by prom mom Melissa Drexler and the case involving Amy Grossberg. However, his letter did not get into evidence.

Jurors were told about the confusion before sentencing, but the appeals court still considered the original testimony legally problematic, especially since it was mentioned in the closing argument. While it's not clear who is to blame for allowing the incorrect testimony to become part of the trial record and jury deliberations, appeals courts are set up for just such occurrences. According to the Associated Press, the appeals court ruled thus: "We conclude that there is reasonable likelihood that Dr. Dietz's false testimony could have affected the judgment of the jury. We further conclude that Dr. Dietz's false testimony affected the substantial rights of appellant."

Prosecutors insisted that the state did not knowingly rely on incorrect testimony, while also pointing out before the panel that Dietz's testimony, even if wrong, was not material to the case, as they had other ways of showing that Yates had planned to kill her children. The appeals court agreed, but since the prosecution had referred to the testimony in making its case, including mentioning it during the closing argument, it may well have influenced the jury's perception.

A New Trial?

Yates could still be tried in the deaths of two of her children, since she was only convicted in the deaths of three. However, a new trial, whether it be for the same deaths again or for those for which she has not yet been tried, may be a crap shoot for either side, and an expensive one at that. The defense has not only learned what did not work three years ago, but they also have access to another high-profile Texas case in which a mother was acquitted by reason of insanity for killing her children at the instigation of supernatural commands.

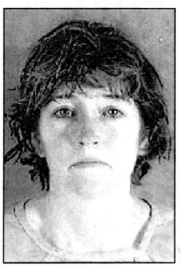

Deanna Laney

Deanna Laney, also evaluated by Park Dietz, stoned her three sons in 2003, two of whom died, because she believed God wanted her to. Dietz found her to be unaware of what she was doing, although she had nowhere near the history of mental illness that Yates had. "She struggled over whether to obey God or to selfishly keep her children," Dietz had testified. His impression was that she had felt she had no choice. Experts scratched their heads over why God's command made a woman insane but the Devil's command did not - especially after Dietz gave an interview to a Virginia newspaper in which he stated that Yates was indeed mentally ill.

While Yates did commit a horrendous crime when she drowned all five of her children, the nation has heard a great deal more since then about both post-partum psychosis and about the problems with the insanity defense. A new jury made up of people possibly exposed to all this information could be quite a different story.

Although Harris County prosecutors say they will appeal the court's decision, legal speculation indicates, according to *Newsweek*, that it's likely to be settled with Yates reassigned to a private mental institution rather than a prison. There she can be properly evaluated. Her husband, Rusty, filed for divorce in July 2004, but hopes the criminal charges will be dropped.

Those who currently care for Yates indicate that she is still considered mentally unstable, and during the fall of 2004, when she was overcome with the horror of what she had done, she had tried to kill herself by refusing to eat, and was hospitalized. A settlement, rather than a trial, may well be in her best interests.

Yet the legal issue remains. While friends and associates of Dietz insist on his integrity and claim that he would not knowingly make a misstatement, one can only wonder why an expert who did not research the information beforehand would testify to it from vague recall. Or why the DA's office did not bother to check its accuracy. Yates's life hung in the balance. She might well have been given the death penalty. Fortunately her attorney ensured that the system worked appropriately.

PART TWO

Susan Smith

Child Murderer or Victim?

The Letter

The beginning of the letter read, "You will, without a doubt, make some lucky man a great wife. But unfortunately, it won't be me." Another passage began, "Susan, I could really fall for you. You have some endearing qualities about you, and I think that you are a terrific person. But like I have told you before, there are some things about you that aren't suited for me, and yes, I am speaking about your children." The letter was a mixture of a "Dear John" letter and a pep talk. The letter was dated October 17, 1994 and was written on a word processor and had the appearance of a formal, business document. The writer was Tom Findlay, 27, the son of the owner of Conso Products, the largest employer in Union, South Carolina. Tom was considered by some to be Unions most eligible bachelor, although when judged strictly on his physical appearance, Tom was average. Tom's hair was thinning and his facial features were indistinct. The letter was addressed to Susan Smith, a secretary at Conso, and a woman Tom Findlay had dated on and off in 1994.

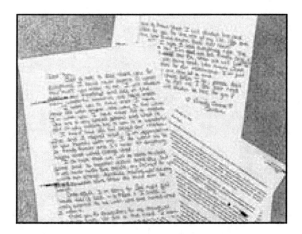

Letters to and from Susan Smith
and Tom Findlay

The tone of the letter was gentle and sections of the letter were flattering toward Susan. Tom wrote that he thought Susan was a great person and that he was impressed that she had enrolled in night school at the local college. Tom encouraged Susan to continue her studies. Tom also wrote that he was proud that Susan was trying to improve her life.

The "Dear John" part of the letter was where Tom explained that he was not Susan's "Mr. Right" because he did not want the responsibility of caring for another man's two small children. Tom also wrote that he was afraid that their backgrounds he was a child of privilege, she was a child of a mill worker who committed suicide when his wife had divorced him were just too far apart. Tom wrote that he was upset by some of Susan's behavior, especially at a hot tub party that he had recently thrown. At that party, Susan and the husband of a friend of Susan's kissed and fondled each other while they were naked in Findlay's hot tub. Findlay wrote, "If you want to catch a nice guy like me one day, you have to act like a nice girl." "And you know, nice girls don't sleep with married men."

Susan was furious at Tom and hurt by his rejection.

The Unthinkable

It was a mild October night in Union. Susan had been driving around for the last hour, trying to calm herself. She drove along Highway 49 and followed the signs to John D. Long Lake. Before driving to the lake on this evening, she had never before been there. Susan preferred to take her sons to the pond at Foster Park, which was closer to her home. At Foster Park, Susan and her sons would feed breadcrumbs to the ducks.

Once she arrived at the shore of John D. Long Lake, Susan drove across a portion of the seventy-five-foot boat ramp and parked in the middle of the ramp. The ramp was unpaved and consisted of gravel and stones. Susan sat quietly behind the wheel of her 1990 burgundy Mazda Protégé, listening to the sounds of her two young sons sleeping. Michael, her oldest son had celebrated his third birthday two weeks earlier and Alex was fourteen months old. Susan was twenty-three, with long, sandy blond hair that she tied in a ponytail. She wore wire-rimmed glasses and was in the best physical shape she had been in since before becoming pregnant with Michael.

Susan Smith

Susan shifted the Mazda into neutral and felt the car slowly begin to roll down the remaining length of the boat ramp. The car only traveled a few yards before Susan stepped on the brake. With a shift tug, Susan pulled the emergency hand brake, stopping the car from further rolling forward. She opened her door and stepped out of the car. Susan stood outside of her car, on the boat ramp, on the banks of John D. Long Lake and thought about suicide. Susan looked around and saw only black. The lake was not illuminated and she stood alone thinking about her life. The darkness and loneliness of the deserted lake mirrored how Susan felt.

Susan wanted relief from her loneliness and the problems in her life. Susan and her husband, David, were in the middle of a divorce and her boyfriend, Tom Findlay, had just rejected her the week before. She wanted to commit suicide, but she did not want her sons to suffer.

Susan believed if she killed her sons first and then committed suicide that her sons would suffer less, rather than if she committed suicide and left them on their own. Yet, something was stopping her from surrendering to her depression and loneliness. She did not want to commit suicide, what she wanted was relief from all the stresses and burdens that overwhelmed her. She felt that her life was filled with loss and rejection, and that the responsibilities of being a single mother were overwhelming.

Susan's next decision will never be forgotten. Attempts to explain it will always fall short and continue to leave the question why? Open to further speculation.

Susan Smith released the emergency brake and softly closed the driver's side door. Michael and Alex were asleep in the back seat, strapped into their car seats. As the car drifted into John D. Long Lake, the headlights were on. The car entered the water slowly and did not submerge immediately. Instead, it remained on the surface, bobbing peacefully, while slowly filling with water

Susan watched the car submerge into the lake. She turned away from the sinking car and began to run toward a small house. The story that Susan would tell would capture the nation's sympathy. Susan's story would also raise doubts in some and cause a community to question some of its own citizens, based solely on the race of those citizens.

After the truth was revealed, many would try to imagine the thoughts running through Susan Smith's head the night of October 25, 1994, when she took the lives of her children. To this day, the question still asked is how could she do it? Susan Smith committed the most unthinkable act when she broke humanity's most sacred trust, the love of a mother for her children.

Susan Leigh Vaughan Smith

Susan Leigh Vaughan Smith was born in Union, South Carolina on September 26, 1971. She was the only daughter born to Linda, a homemaker, and Harry, a firefighter who later worked in one of the textile mills that surrounded Union.

Union, South Carolina is in Union County and both the city and the county received their names from the old Union Church that stood a short distance from the Monarch Mill. When it was first founded, Union was known as Unionville; later it was shortened to Union. The county's first white settlers came from Virginia in 1749. Union County's population grew the fastest between 1762 and the start of the Revolutionary War. Settlers built log cabins and cultivated tobacco, flax, corn and wheat. Union was one of the first towns settled in the area and was untouched during the Civil War because the Broad River flooded and turned Sherman's troops away from the town.

Today, Union County has a population of 30,300. The city of Union, the county's largest town, has a population of 9,800. 69.8% of the population of Union County is Caucasian and 29.9% is African American. Union County includes several smaller towns: Lockhart, Carlisle and Buffalo. There are many industrial and manufacturing plants located in these towns which employ 13,000 people. A large portion of Union County is part of Sumter National Forest.

The per capita income in the town of Union is $9,230; the median family income is $25,760 and the median household income is $18,790. Downtown Union is composed of a shopping area, four shopping centers and a branch of the University of South Carolina. Union is also home to the first Carnegie Library in South Carolina.

Linda, Susan's mother

In 1960, Harry Ray Vaughan was twenty and Linda was seventeen and pregnant from a previous relationship when they married. Together, Harry and Linda had a son, Scotty, a daughter, Susan and they raised Linda's son, Michael. Harry and Linda's marriage had many conflicts and some of those conflicts escalated to the point where Harry became violent and threatened to kill Linda and then him. Harry's violence was the result of his alcoholism and his obsession with the idea that Linda was unfaithful. During Susan's early childhood, her home life was very dysfunctional.

The turmoil in the Vaughan's household caused Susan and her older brother Scotty to be very frightened. They were especially frightened by the behavior of their parents toward one another. Before Susan entered preschool, her half-brother, Michael, tried to commit suicide by hanging himself. Michael was treated at Duke University Medical

Center and at other residential treatment facilities during Susan's childhood. As a result of her turbulent home life, Susan was an unhappy child. The mother of one of her playmates described Susan as unusual and sad. Susan would stare in space, like she wasn't there.

Although Susan was a sad child, she was especially close to her father and would light up whenever Harry was around. In 1977, after seventeen years of marriage, Linda divorced Harry. Susan was six years old. Harry was devastated by the divorce; he became even more depressed and continued to drink heavily.

On January 15, 1978, five weeks after Harry and Linda's divorce became final, Harry Vaughan committed suicide. The suicide was preceded by an argument that Harry and Linda had that escalated and forced Linda to call the police. When the police officers arrived at Linda's house, they saw Harry strike Linda. The police report also noted that Harry had broken a window to gain entry into Linda's home. After the police came to Linda's home, Harry apparently feared that he would hurt someone and appealed to one of the police officers to take him to court so that he could have himself jailed.

Harry committed suicide by placing a gun between his legs and aiming the gun at his abdomen. Harry then pulled the trigger, mortally wounding himself, but he did not die immediately. Harry called 911 for assistance and was rushed to the hospital, but emergency surgery could not save his life. Harry was thirty-seven years old when he died.

Harry's suicide left a huge void in Susan's life. During her childhood, Susan would treasure two possessions: Harrys coin collection and a tape recording of his voice.

Beverly (Bev) Russell

Two weeks after her divorce from Harry became final;
Linda married Beverly (Bev) Russell, a well-to-do
businessman who owned an appliance store in downtown
Union. Bev had been previously married and had several
daughters from his first marriage.

Bev had once been a Democrat, but had switched to the
Republican Party, becoming a South Carolina State
Republican executive committeeman and a member of the
advisory board of the Christian Coalition.

After her mother's remarriage, Susan and her brothers
moved from the Vaughan's modest home outside of Union,
into Bev's three bedroom home in the exclusive Mount
Vernon Estates section of Union.

Susan did well in school. Throughout her elementary,
junior and high school years, Susan excelled. While she
was in high school, she was a member of the Beta Club, a
club for students with a grade point average of B or better.
She also was a member of the Math, Spanish and Red
Cross Clubs. Susan volunteered in Unions annual Special

Olympics and worked with the elderly. Susan was named president of the Junior Civitan Club, a high school club that performed volunteer work in the community, and from 1986 to 1988, Susan and her best friend, Donna Garner, volunteered as candy stripers at Wallace Thompson Hospital in Union.

During Susan's senior year of high school in 1989, she was voted Friendliest Female at Union High School. Susan's classmates remembered her as cheerful and down to earth. Although she was a bit chubby in high school, Susan wore miniskirts and blouses which flattered her figure. Susan was vivacious and outgoing, but this only masked her insecurity and burning need for male attention.

Despite Susan's record of achievement and her image as a model daughter and friend, Susan's life was filled with turmoil. Some of it came from her relationship with her stepfather. Over the years, Bev's attention and approval became increasingly important to Susan and she found herself competing with her mother for his attention.

In 1987, when Susan was about to celebrate her sixteenth birthday, one of Bev's daughters from his previous marriage stayed overnight in the Russell home. The daughter was given Susan's bedroom and Susan was to sleep on the family room sofa. When Susan was ready to go to sleep, Bev was sitting at one end of the sofa. Rather than ask Bev to move, Susan crawled into Bev's lap and began to fall asleep. It was odd for a fifteen-year-old to act like a two-year-old, but Susan may have felt that this behavior was harmless. Bev, on the other hand, seemed to feel that Susan's behavior was provocative. Susan fell asleep, but gradually awoke to the awareness of Bev's hand moving slowly yet firmly from her shoulder to her breasts. Bev then took Susan's hand and placed it directly on his genitals.

Susan pretended to be asleep while the molestation took place. Susan later told her mother that she did not object to Bev's behavior because she wanted to see how far he would go. Susan's response was clearly inappropriate.

Susan filed a complaint against Bev that was investigated by the South Carolina Department of Social Services and the Union County sheriff's office. Linda contacted Susan's guidance counselor and obtained the name of a family counselor. Bev, Linda and Susan only went for family counseling four or five times before discontinuing the sessions. While the matter was being investigated, Bev agreed to move out of the family's home, but returned a short time later.

During Susan's murder trial, it was revealed that the abuse never stopped. According to Seymour Halleck, the defenses psychiatric expert, the family seemed to blame Susan as much as Bev. The family was concerned that stories about the sexual abuse would spread into the community and they blamed Susan for worsening the situation by making it public and reporting it to the Department of Social Services.

In February 1988, Susan was seventeen and sought out her guidance counselor, Camille Stribling for advice. Susan told Stribling that her stepfather had been molesting her. Stribling was required by law to report the sexual abuse allegations to the South Carolina State Department of Social Services. An official in that department called the Union County sheriff's office.

Records from the Union County sheriff's office indicate that in March 1988, Susan reported an incident of sexual molestation by her stepfather to her high school guidance counselor and to her mother. Linda told officials from the sheriff's office that when she confronted Bev, he had not denied that the incident of abuse had occurred. The Department of Social Services sent a caseworker to interview Susan, Susan's guidance counselor and several of Susan's teachers.

At Susan's trial, the caseworker testified that she had learned that Bev Russell had on repeated occasions, fondled Susan's breasts on top of her clothing, French-kissed her and had taken Susan's hand and placed it on his genitals.

No charges were brought against Bev Russell regarding this second series of molestation acts and there was no court hearing because Susan, probably under pressure from Linda, agreed not to press any charges against Bev. The Department of Social Services caseworker did not let the matter drop so easily and notified Assistant Circuit Solicitor Jack Flynn. The caseworker tried to convince Flynn to take the matter to court in order to obtain a court order so that charges of assault and battery of a high and aggravated nature could be brought against Bev. However, an agreement was reached between Robert Guess, Bev's attorney, and Solicitor Flynn and charges were never filed against Bev. The agreement reached by Guess and Flynn was presented to Judge David Wilburn on March 25, 1988. Judge Wilburn sealed the agreement, which meant that the agreement would never be made available to the public.

Susan Smith's high school yearbook photo, 1988

In the summer of 1988, between her junior and senior years of high school, Susan began working at the Winn-Dixie supermarket in Union. Susan's first job at the market was as a cashier, but within six months she was promoted to head cashier and later she was promoted again and became the markets bookkeeper. At the beginning of her senior year in high school, Susan began to secretly date one of her co-workers from Winn-Dixie, an older married man. Shortly after her relationship with the older, married co-worker began. Susan became pregnant and had an abortion. At the same time that this relationship was occurring, Susan was also dating another co-worker. After the abortion, the older married co-worker found out about the other relationship, and ended his relationship with Susan. Susan became deeply depressed over the breakup. In early November 1988, Susan attempted to commit suicide by taking an overdose of aspirin and Tylenol. Susan was admitted to the Spartanburg Regional Medical Center on November 7, 1988 and remained hospitalized for one week. During her hospitalization, Susan's doctors discovered that this was not Susan's first suicide attempt. When Susan was thirteen years old, she had taken a similar overdose of aspirin. Susan spent a month recovering from her suicide attempt. The managers of Winn-Dixie were supportive and allowed Susan to return to her job.

Prior to her suicide attempt, Susan became friendly with David Smith, one of the stock clerks at Winn-Dixie. Susan knew David because they had attended Union High School together at the same time. During the time Susan was involved in her two relationships, David was dating his longtime girlfriend, Christy Jennings. David and Susan became friendly and when Susan returned from her month long recovery, David broke up with Christy and began to pursue a relationship with Susan.

David Smith

Barbara, David's mother

David Smith was born on July 27, 1970, the second of three children born to Barbara and Charles David Smith. Charles Smith was also called David and was a Navy veteran who had served two tours of duty in Vietnam. Barbara Smith was a devout Jehovah's Witness who sheltered David from many outside influences during his childhood. When David was two years old, the Smith family moved from Royal Oak, Michigan to Putnam, five miles northwest of Union. David's father worked in a clothing store in downtown Union and later as manager of Wal-Mart. While David was growing up, his mother had two part-time jobs: she worked in a lawyer's office and in a dialysis clinic. David's mother also attended college part-time and studied to be a nurse. David had an older stepbrother, Billy, from his mother's first marriage, an older brother, Danny and a younger sister, Becky.

David's parents' marriage was troubled. Over the years of their marriage, David's father grew to dislike his wife and her devotion to her religion. As David grew older, he found the strict religious practices of his mother's religion and its insistence on isolation from the larger community distasteful. In David's longtime girlfriend Christy Jennings opinion, David's childhood was difficult and deprived. David followed his father's example and rejected the Jehovah's Witnesses. This caused friction within the Smith household and when David was seventeen, he distanced himself further from his mother and moved out of his parent's home and into his great-grandmother, Forest Moner Malone's home next door. David's older brother Danny was also living at their great-grandmothers house.

At the age of sixteen, David began working after school at Winn-Dixie. David was an average student, but he had a very strong work ethic and was a pleasant and personable young man.

David Smith's 1988 high school yearbook photo

During the summer of 1990, David and Susan began to date, although at the time, David was engaged to Christy

Jennings. David viewed his relationship with Susan as casual and not serious. In January 1991, after dating for about a year, Susan found out she was pregnant. David told Christy about Susan and Christy broke off her relationship with David immediately.

David and Susan decided to get married because they were both against Susan having an abortion. Although marriage represented safety and stability to Susan, it also meant that she would have to give up her plans to attend college. Susan desired to go to college, but she really had no idea what college she wanted to attend or what she wanted to study.

In their own ways, Susan and David were emotionally needy people who found comfort and in the beginning of their relationship, similarities with each other. David and Susan seemed to fulfill what the other needed emotionally; however their relationship was filled with many stresses and strains. Susan and David's backgrounds were completely different and this also caused friction between them. David was raised in the country and Susan was raised in the city. In Union, the city kids like Susan looked down on the country kids like David.

Susan's mother and stepfather were not pleased by the news of Susan's pregnancy and marriage. Susan's mother was disappointed that David did not have a college education and was not from the same economic background as Susan.

On March 4, 1991, David's older brother, Danny who was twenty-two, died of complications from Crohn's disease, a painful inflammation of the intestinal tract. During the winter of 1991, Danny had undergone surgery at the Spartanburg Regional Medical Center. After the surgery,

Danny developed a bacterial infection and, in his already weakened condition, quickly deteriorated and died. Eleven days later on March 15, 1991, Susan and David wed at the United Methodist Church in Bogansville. Susan was nineteen and two months pregnant. David was twenty. Even though David's family was dealing with the death of Danny, Susan's mother, Linda, insisted that the wedding go forward as scheduled. Linda was concerned that Susan's pregnancy would begin to show before the wedding could take place.

David had worked steadily over several years renovating a small house located on the same property as his great grandmother's house. Before Susan and David were married, David had shown Susan the house and told her of his plans for living in the house after they were married. In David's eyes, Susan had agreed with him that they would live in the house after they were married, but those plans changed when Bev and Linda saw the house. Susan lost interest in living in the house after her parents visit. To David, the simple country home was comfortable and ideal for his and Susan's needs. To Susan, it was a "tin-roofed country shack." Susan probably dreamed of moving into a new home that was bigger and grander than the home she had been raised in. Susan and David compromised, and Susan moved in with David at Moner's house.

In May 1991, three months after Susan and David's wedding, David's father attempted to commit suicide. Susan found him at his home on the floor. David's father had taken an overdose of pills. From the strain of Danny's death and David's fathers attempted suicide, David's parents' marriage fell apart. David's mother, Barbara, moved to Garden City, South Carolina, near Myrtle Beach. David's father continued to live in Putnam. After his suicide attempt, David's father was hospitalized and treated for depression. During his hospitalization, David's father met Sue, the woman who would become his second wife.

Family Life

Susan worked at Winn-Dixie until she went into labor. Michael Daniel Smith was born on October 10, 1991 at Mary Black Hospital in Spartanburg. Michael's middle name was chosen in honor of David's brother, Danny. After Michaels birth, Susan continued to work part-time at Winn-Dixie and enrolled in several college courses at the branch of the University of South Carolina in Union.

Early in their marriage, David and Susan felt a great deal of tension. The tension and trouble was no surprise to their friends. In Union, it was customary for young people to marry after finishing high school and then begin to have children. Young couples often found themselves with demands and responsibilities that exceed their expectations of married life. One of the areas that caused tension between David and Susan was money. According to David, Susan was always interested in material things. Susan also worried about paying the bills and often asked her mother for loans. This angered David. David and Susan earned a fairly good income; David earned about $22,000 a year and Susan earned about $17,000 during the years that they were married.

Another area of tension in Susan and David's marriage was Linda and David's relationship. Linda and David did not get along with one another. Linda was very controlling and would often visit the Smiths without calling first. Linda often offered unsolicited advice and opinions about how David and Susan were raising Michael and how to deal with problems in their marriage. According to David, Susan seemed to almost always follow what Linda said.

Another stress on their marriage was the fact that Susan and David both worked at Winn-Dixie. At Winn-Dixie, David was Susan's boss. Another problem with David and Susan's marriage was their extramarital affairs. By their third wedding anniversary, David and Susan had separated several times. David moved between Moner's house and the Smiths house on Toney Road frequently.

During their first separation in March 1992, shortly after their one-year wedding anniversary, Susan rekindled a relationship with a former boyfriend at Winn-Dixie and this angered David.

During another separation in the summer of 1992, Susan and Michael lived at Linda and Bev's home. David and Susan tried to mend their relationship and throughout 1992, David and Susan's relationship seesawed back and forth. Susan became pregnant in November 1992. In December, David and Susan decided to try again to live under the same roof. Susan told David that the only chance their relationship had to succeed was if they had their own home. In the winter of 1993, David and Susan brought a small ranch style house with dark red shutters at 407 Toney Road in Union. Bev and Linda provided the down payment.

Susan's second pregnancy was not as happy an experience as her first with Michael. David remembers that Susan complained non-stop about becoming "fat and ugly." Slowly, Susan began to shut David out of her life. She complained about the physical aspects of their relationship and stopped sharing anecdotes about Michael with David.

David became lonely and wanted someone to talk to. In June 1993, David began a relationship with a cashier at Winn-Dixie, Tiffany Moss. Susan and Tiffany had attended high school together at the same time. They were not

friends, but they knew each other. Susan was jealous of
David. Employees at Winn-Dixie remember incidents when
Susan would visit David and scream at him when she saw
David talking to women in the store.

Michael and Alexander

Susan and David's second son Alexander Tyler was born
on August 5, 1993. Susan had an emergency Cesarean
section. After Alex's birth, Susan and David put aside their
differences for a short time in order to settle their new baby
at home and allow Susan time to heal from her Cesarean.
Within three weeks of Alex's birth, Susan and David
decided that their relationship was over and David moved
out of the Toney Road house and into Moner's house.
Although Susan and David's marriage was troubled and
headed for divorce, by all accounts, Susan and David were
devoted parents who adored their children.

After recovering from Alex's birth, Susan found a new job
at Conso Products. Susan decided that she could not return

to Winn-Dixie because she was not getting along with David, who would be her supervisor. Nor did she want to work in the same place as David's girlfriend, Tiffany Moss.

Susan was hired as a bookkeeper at Conso Products and eventually became the assistant to the executive secretary for J. Carey Findlay, the president and CEO of Conso. Findlay was an accountant from Charlotte, North Carolina, who bought Conso in 1986 with a group of investors. They had originally planned to reorganize Conso and turn around and sell the company for a quick profit, but Findlay was excited by the business and bought out his partners in 1988. Findlay settled permanently in Union and purchased an estate seven miles south of Union. In November 1993, Conso Products announced a public offering of its stock, becoming the first publicly owned corporation in Union. At the end of 1993, Conso had factories in Great Britain, Canada and Mexico.

Susan enjoyed working at Conso. She liked the responsibilities she had handling hotel arrangements for out-of-town clients, ordering flowers and arranging for Findlay's travel. Susan was exposed to elements of an expensive lifestyle were foreign to her. Susan also enjoyed working at Conso for another reason: Tom Findlay. Tom was one of three sons of J. Carey Findlay. Tom was twenty-seven and had grown up in an upscale suburb of Birmingham, Alabama. Tom had graduated with a bachelor's degree from Auburn University in 1990 and had moved to Union to work as the head of the graphic arts department of Conso. Tom was responsible for designing and producing Consos brochures. He was popular with young women in Union, because he was young, rich and available.

Conso also provided Susan with a new group of friends and Susan spent a lot of time socializing with them at Unions only bar, Hickory Nuts, which opened during the summer of 1993.

During Susan and David's last separation before Susan filed for divorce, Tom and Susan began to date. Beginning in January 1994 and for a period of several months, Susan and Tom frequently met for lunch or went to the movies. Susan visited Tom at his cottage on his father's estate and attended several parties thrown by Tom there.

During the spring and early summer of 1994, Susan and David tried one final time to make their marriage work. David moved back to the Toney Road house and stopped seeing Tiffany. During this time Susan and Tom had broken off their relationship as well. At the end of July 1994, Susan told David that she wanted a divorce. David had wanted the marriage to work, especially because he believed his sons needed their mother and father together.

In August, David rented a two-bedroom apartment in the Lakeside Gardens complex about two miles from the house Susan, Michael and Alex lived in on Toney Road. David brought new furniture for his apartment and set up a bedroom with a bed, a crib and new toys for Michael and Alex.

At the beginning of September, Susan began to believe that her life was finally settling down. She and David had an amicable relationship centered on taking care of their sons and Susan was beginning to believe that her dreams of love and stability might be realized with Tom Findlay, who she had begun to date again in September. However, Tom Findlay had different ideas. Tom liked Susan but he ended their relationship because he began to feel that Susan was too possessive and too needy.

On September 21st, Susan's attorney served divorce papers on David. Susan sought a divorce on the grounds of adultery. On October 21st, Susans divorce papers were filed at the Union county courthouse; several days earlier she had received Tom Findlay's "Dear John" letter. Susan was furious and she sought Tom out at his cottage on Sunday, October 23 in the hope of restoring her relationship with him. Susan tried to gain Toms sympathy by telling him about her sexual relationship with Bev Russell, but this only seemed to shock Tom.

The Big Lie

The fall of 1994 had been full of activity for Susan. She worked full time at Conso, managed a part time college course load at the University of South Carolina, had custody of her two toddler sons and was sexually involved with three men: Bev Russell, Tom Findlay and her estranged husband, David. Increasingly, Susan was filled with anxiety and when she was alone, she became deeply depressed. During this period of time, Susan had begun to take days off from work to drink. This was unusual behavior for her.

Tuesday, October 25, 1994 began like any other day for Susan Smith. Susan dressed and fed her children breakfast and then drove them to daycare. Susan went to work and at lunch joined a group of Conso employees, one of whom was Tom Findlay, at a restaurant in Buffalo. While the group laughed and talked, Susan sat quietly. At around 1:30 p.m., Susan asked her supervisor, Sandy Williams, if she could leave work early. Sandy asked Susan if something was wrong and Susan confided in Sandy that she was upset because she was "in love with someone who doesn't love me." Sandy asked Susan who that person was and Susan replied, "Tom Findlay, but it can never be because of my children." Rather than go home, Susan remained at her desk.

Tom Findlay

At around 2:30 p.m., Susan called Tom in his office to ask him to meet her outside of the building to talk. Susan told Tom that David was threatening to expose and make public some embarrassing information about her in their divorce proceedings. Tom asked her to explain what the information was and Susan told Tom that David would accuse her of cheating the IRS and of having an affair with your father. After recovering from the shock of hearing about this alleged affair, Tom told Susan that their friendship would remain intact, but that our intimate relationship will have to stop forever.

At 4:30 p.m., Susan sought out Tom again in the Conso photography studio. Susan attempted to return Toms

Auburn University sweatshirt that she had borrowed, but Tom refused to accept it. Tom told Susan to hold on to it.

After collecting her sons at day care, Susan headed in her car to Hickory Nuts; while she was driving there she spotted Sue Brown, the marketing manager at Conso, in her car. Both Sue and Susan pulled into the Hickory Nuts parking lot. Susan talked to Sue and convinced her to return to Conso with her so that she could apologize to Tom for lying to him about sleeping with his father. Susan had concocted the story in order to see Tom's reaction to it. The woman arrived at Conso around 5:30 p.m. Susan wanted Sue to watch her children while she spoke to Tom. Tom was not happy to see Susan and quickly led her out of his office. Susan told Sue Brown that she was upset after talking to Tom and that she may just end it. Sandy Williams was leaving Conso for the day when she spotted Susan Smith and Sue Brown in the parking lot. Sandy felt manipulated and deceived by Susan who had insisted that she could not stay at work and had to go home because she was so upset by her boyfriend's rejection. Susan dropped Sue Brown off at Later in the evening; Sue Brown was eating dinner at Hickory Nuts with several friends, including Tom Findlay. During the meal, a waiter brought a cordless telephone to Sue. Susan Smith was calling to ask Sue if Tom Findlay had asked about her. Sue told Susan that he had not.

At 8:00 p.m., Susan dressed her sons, placed them in their car seats in her car and began driving around Union. Susan later described her reaction to Tom's rejection by saying that she had never felt so lonely and sad in my entire life.

Hickory Nuts and drove home; it was about 6:00 p.m.

Around 9:00 p.m., Shirley McCloud was relaxing in the living room of her home, located about one quarter mile from John D. Long Lake. Shirley was just finishing Tuesdays *Union Daily Times* when she heard a wailing sound coming from her front porch. Shirley switched on the porch light and saw a young woman sobbing hysterically. The young woman cried, Please help me! He's got my kids and he's got my car. Shirley led Susan Smith into her home and Susan told her, A black man has got my kids and my car. Shirley's husband, Rick told his son Rick, Jr. to call 911.

At 9:12 p.m., the 911 dispatcher called the Union County sheriff's office to direct them to respond to the Rick McCloud's 911 call. Once Susan had calmed down, Shirley asked Susan to tell her what happened. Susan told her the following story: I was stopped at the red light at Monarch Mills and a black man jumped in and told me to drive. I asked him why he was doing this and he said shut up and drive or I'll kill you. Susan continued and told Shirley that, at the abductors direction; she drove northeast of Union for about four miles until, he made me stop right past the sign. Shirley confirmed that the sign was for the John D. Long Lake, which was located several hundred yards outside of Shirley's front door. He told me to get out. He made me stop in the middle of the road. Nobody was coming, not a single car. Susan continued, I asked him, why can't I take my kids? Susan told Shirley that the man said, I don't have time. Susan said that the man pushed her out of her car while he was pointing a gun at her side. Susan continued by telling Shirley that When he finally got me out he said, Don't worry, I'm not going to hurt your kids.

Susan described how she had laid on the ground as the man drove away as both of her sons cried out for their mother. After a while, Susan wasn't sure how long, she began to run and stopped when she reached Shirley McCloud's porch. Susan asked Shirley if she could use the bathroom and if she could call her mother. When Susan was unable to reach her mother, she called her stepfather and then her husband, David at Winn-Dixie. By the time Susan reached David by phone, the Union County Sheriff, Howard Wells had driven to the McCloud's home and was directing the search for the Smith children.

David comforts Susan

Sheriff Wells knew Susan through his friendship with Susan's brother, Scotty and Scotty's wife, Wendy. Wells and his wife Wanda considered themselves close friends of Scotty and Wendy Vaughn. Wells asked Susan to repeat her story, although he had heard it from the 911 dispatcher and from Shirley McCloud. Wells took notes and asked Susan questions. Wells noted that Susan was wearing a gray sweatshirt with orange lettering spelling out Auburn University. Susan's face was red and puffy and her hands rested in her lap. Susan described the clothes that her sons were wearing. Michael was wearing a white jogging suit and Alex was wearing a red and white-striped outfit. After Susan finished, Wells realized that the carjacking was not going to be solved quickly nor would the Union County sheriff's office have all the resources necessary to find the Smith children. Wells called Chief Robert Stewart, the head of South Carolina Law Enforcement Division, known by the initials, SLED, for additional assistance.

Wells did not question the information Susan had provided to him or her story. Wells was concerned with collecting all the available information and following whatever leads developed. As time passed and more scrutiny could be applied to the information he had collected, Wells could begin to sort out fact from fiction.

The Investigation

Union County sheriff's deputies continued searching for the Smith brothers and Susan's Mazda while Susan, David and the Vaughn-Russell families gathered at the McClouds' home. Around midnight, Sheriff Wells suggested that Susan and her family find another meeting place. Susan volunteered her mother's home and Susan, David, Bev, Linda and assorted friends and family left the McCloud's for the Russell home. Susan rode with David in his car to the Russell's. On the way to the Russell's, Susan told David that Tom Findlay might come and see her and that she didn't want David to become angry. David found Susan's statement incredible in light of the fact that their sons were missing. It seemed that Susan was more worried that David would become upset if her boyfriend came to visit, rather than worrying about finding their sons.

Wells returned to his office and began to organize the investigation. He called SLED to coordinate efforts to send divers to John D. Long Lake to search the lake. A SLED helicopter with heat sensors flew over John D. Long Lake and nearby Sumter National Forest. Divers who searched the lake did not find anything on the bottom of John D. Long Lake in the area they searched. Wells needed to obtain a better; more detailed description of the kidnapper from Susan and made arrangements for a police sketch artist to sketch a composite drawing. The police artist met with Susan and using the description she provided composed a sketch of a black man, around forty years of age, wearing a dark knit cap, a dark shirt, jeans and a plaid jacket.

Throughout October 26, 1994, Union County sheriff deputies and SLED agents searched the area surrounding

John D. Long Lake. Agents conducted interviews of the McCloud family. Another organization also became involved in the search for Michael and Alex Smith, the Adam Walsh Center, located in the state capitol, Columbia, about 70 miles south of Union. The Adam Walsh Center was named in memory of six-year-old Adam Walsh who disappeared during a shopping trip with his mother from a Florida Sears store in 1981. Even though an intense search was undertaken to find Adam, he remained missing for ten days until his body was found 150 miles from where he had disappeared. Adams killer was never found. In 1981 law enforcement agencies did not have standard operating procedures for locating missing children. There were no computer databases of child molesters, no clearinghouses of information on missing children, and no way for one law enforcement agency to communicate with another. John and Reve Walsh, Adams parents, dedicated themselves to changing the system. As a result of their efforts, the 1984 Missing Children's Act was passed. The act organized a computerized system for sharing information and established four regional missing children centers in the United States, one of which was located in Columbia.

Later in the afternoon of October 26th, Margaret Frierson, Executive Director of the South Carolina Chapter of the Adam Walsh Center spoke to Susan's sister-in-law, Wendy Vaughn, and offered the centers assistance to Susan and David Smith. Margaret told Wendy that she would need to speak to Susan and David and asked that they call her back. They never did. Instead, Bev Russell called Margaret later that same day and provided directions to his home. Before driving to Union, Margaret and her assistant, Charlotte Foster, worked with SLED to obtain pictures of Michael and Alex and arranged for fliers to be printed describing the missing boys.

Susan and David continued to stay with Bev and Linda Russell. David's father and his wife Sue flew to Union from California and David's uncle Doug and his wife drove from Michigan to be with him. The house quickly filled with other relatives, friends, neighbors and ministers. Susan never spent a moment alone. In her parents' home, her friends and family comforted Susan and provided the affectionate nurturing Susan so badly desired. This was in sharp contrast to the isolation and loneliness she recently felt.

Tom Findlay called Susan and expressed his sympathies about Michael and Alex. Susan shifted the topic of conversation away from her missing children and to her relationship with him. Tom told Susan not to worry about their relationship and to concentrate on her children. This telephone call would be the only one that Susan would receive from Tom. Tom never visited Susan, not even when a group of Susan's co-workers from Conso visited. When Sue Brown came to visit, Susan Smith asked her when Tom was planning to visit her.

Margaret Frierson and Charlotte Foster arrived at the Russell home on the afternoon of October 26th. Instead of talking to Susan and David alone, as they preferred, the women met with Susan, David, Bev, Linda and Scotty Vaughn. Margaret explained why the Adam Walsh Center was founded and what services it could provide to the parents of missing children. Margaret explained that she and Charlotte could act as the family's liaison with the news media and could arrange and schedule interviews and broadcast pictures of the missing boys and information about the crime. After 40 minutes, Susan and David excused themselves from the conversation and drove to the sheriff's office for interviews. Margaret followed David and Susan in her car. Sheriff Wells questioned Susan in his office. Margaret and SLED investigator Eddie Harris spoke with David about making a plea for the safe return of his sons to the news media. Margaret and Harris believed that a nationally televised appeal for the children's return would be instrumental in solving the boy's disappearance. David was nervous, but agreed that it was important to do anything that would return his sons.

The news media descended in large numbers on Union. At first the carjacking was covered by the local paper, the *Union Daily Times;* and local radio stations, but interest in the story quickly grew and the national networks were soon covering the story.

David, with Susan by his side, stood on the steps of the Union County Sheriff's department and made the following statement: "To whoever has our boys, we ask that you please don't hurt them and bring them back. We love them very much...I plead to the guy please return our children to us safe and unharmed. Everywhere I look, I see their play toys and pictures. They are both wonderful children. I don't know how else to put it. And I can't imagine life without them." After he finished David, along with Susan, returned to the sheriff's office. Susan was questioned by both investigators from the Union County sheriff's office and agents from SLED for about six hours. Susan was asked on a number of occasions to repeat the details of her story.

At the end of the day, Sheriff Wells called David A. Caldwell, Director of the Forensic Sciences Laboratory for the State Law Enforcement Division in Columbia and asked him to drive to Union to interview Susan Smith.

Two days after the carjacking, on Thursday, October 27, 1994, both David and Susan submitted to polygraph tests administered by the FBI. Susan and David each read and signed a form advising them of their Miranda rights, their right to remain silent, their right to an attorney, and their right to stop talking to investigators. David's test showed that he knew nothing about the disappearance of his sons. Susan's test was inconclusive. Susan's test showed that her greatest level of deception was when she was asked the question; "Do you know where your children are?" The investigators did not hide the results of her polygraph from Susan. Susan told David that she thought she had not done well on the test. She wasn't sure that she failed the test outright, but she told David that she thought the police might begin to doubt her story. This would be the first of many polygraph tests Susan was given. Each time Susan was interviewed, she was given a polygraph test. This would be the one and only polygraph test given to David.

There were several inconsistencies in Susan's story. Over the course of the day, Agent Caldwell interviewed Susan on three separate occasions at the Union County sheriff's office. Agent Caldwell asked Susan to relate the details of October 25, beginning when she awoke in the morning until she spoke with Sheriff Wells at the McClouds' house. Susan told Caldwell she had called her mother after she came home from work to ask if she could visit her later in the evening. Susan's mother told her that she had other plans and would not be home. Susan made dinner for her sons, but they were fussy and did not want to eat. David called Susan during the time she was preparing dinner and later told the police that he could hear his sons in the background and that they seemed "fussy". Susan told Caldwell that at 7:30 p.m., Michael told her he wanted to go to Wal-Mart. Caldwell questioned Susan about this and Susan admitted that she suggested going to Wal-Mart. Susan told Caldwell she drove to Foster Park and stayed until 8:40 p.m., but did not get out of her car. Susan then claimed she returned to the Wal-Mart parking lot because of the bright lights so that she could search for Alex's bottle that he had dropped on the floor of the car. Susan then told Caldwell that Michael had suggested visiting Mitchell Sinclair, fiance of her best friend Donna Garner, but then amended her answer when Caldwell questioned her further about it. Susan told Caldwell that Mitch lived less than a mile north of the Monarch intersection and that she had stopped at a red light on Monarch, but saw no other cars at the intersection while she had stopped.

Agent Caldwell told Susan that investigators had spoken to Mitchell and he told them that he had not been expecting her and that he wasn't home around 9:00 p.m. Agent Caldwell also told Susan that investigators had visited the Wal-Mart and had spoken to many people who were working or shopping in the store that evening and that no one remembered seeing Susan or her two children. Susan backpedaled away from her story and said that she had actually been driving around for hours with her two children strapped to their car seats. Susan had not said anything about this to investigators because she was afraid that her behavior sounded suspicious.

After interviewing Susan on October 26, investigators became suspicious of her story. The light at the Monarch intersection is permanently green unless a car on the cross street triggers the signal to switch. If there had been no other cars on the road that night, the light would not have been red.

While Agent Caldwell was interviewing Susan, David met with other SLED investigators and told them that Susan had been dating other men. The investigators wanted names and dates. David told them about Tom Findlay. David was frustrated that the investigators were focusing so much attention on Susan rather than searching for his sons. Agent

Caldwell told Susan that investigators had obtained information that Susan had a boyfriend, Tom Findlay, and that Tom had broken off his relationship with Susan because of Susan's sons. Caldwell asked Susan, "Did this fact play any role or have any bearing on the disappearance of your children?" Susan replied that, "No man would make me hurt my children. They were my life." Susan's answer indicated that she thought her sons were no longer alive.

Later in the day, when Susan was interviewed again by Agent Caldwell, she was confronted again by the inconsistencies in her story. Agent Caldwell demanded to know why Susan had not told the truth about Wal-Mart. Caldwell asked Susan about her children's fussiness and asked Susan, "is that why you killed them?" Susan slammed her fist on the table and said, "You son of a b-! How can you think that?" Susan got up from her chair and left the office where the interview was taking place yelling, "I can't believe that you think I did it!"

Agent Caldwell noted that from time to time during his interview with Susan, she would sob, but tears would not always accompany her apparent crying. The FBI agent, who administered her polygraph test on October 27, noted that Susan made "fake sounds of crying with no tears in her eyes."

Another person who thought Susan was lying about the carjacking was the forensic artist, Roy Paschal, who had drawn the sketch of the carjacker from Susan's description. Paschal felt that Susan was vague in her description of the kidnapper, but she was very specific about some of the small details in the drawing.

Sketch of the alleged abductor

Sheriff Wells and Agent Logan contacted the FBI's
Behavioral Sciences Unit for assistance. Wells and Logan
asked the unit to provide a profile of the characteristics of a
homicidal mother. The profile the FBI provided fit Susan
Smith almost perfectly.

The FBI's profile described a woman in her twenties, who
grew up or lived in poverty, was under-educated, had a
history of either physical or sexual abuse or both, remained
isolated from social supports, had depressive and suicidal
tendencies and was usually experiencing rejection by a
male lover at the time she murdered. The profile also
described how the mother might also find herself enmeshed
with her children and show an inability to define her
boundaries as separate from her children. The profile also
described how depression in the mother was often
correlated with a blurring of boundaries. A mothers
biological ties, her strong role expectations to be a mother,
her significantly greater care giving responsibilities, her
isolation in carrying out those responsibilities and her

greater tendency toward depression and self-destruction were likely to result in her becoming trapped in enmeshment with her children.

During a homicidal act, a mother may view a child as a mere extension of herself rather than as a separate being. A mother's suicidal inclination may often be transformed into filial homicide.

The investigation continued into its third day. Sheriff Wells appeared on the *Today* show and on *Larry King Live*. He told Larry King that his office had received more than 1,000 calls but that none had developed into a strong lead to follow. Divers searched the bottom of John D. Long Lake, but they found nothing in the murky water.

Experts had made a tremendous error when they told the divers to assume that anyone trying to hide a car would drive it into the water at a high rate of speed. None of the experts considered that a driver might simply let a car roll from the edge of the banks into the water. It is easy to envision that a car driven into a body of water at a high speed would go further than a car driven slowly, in reality, the opposite occurs. The faster that a car hits the water, the more waves it creates which stops the forward momentum of the car. A car driven at a high rate of speed into water simply drops and sinks at the edge of the body of water. Because the Mazda had been rolled into the lake at a slow speed, it had drifted out much further from the edge of the water, nearly 100 feet. Drivers searched the edge of the water, while the Mazda remained submerged.

On Friday morning, October 28, 50 volunteer fire fighters and dozens of SLED agents and sheriff's deputies searched the north and south sides of Highway 49 near John D. Long Lake. They came up empty handed. Sheriff Wells held a press conference to announce that he had no solid clues in the kidnapping of Michael and Alex and he had not ruled out any suspects, including Susan and David Smith. Wells also stated that the investigators had uncovered several discrepancies in Susan's statements, but Wells would not elaborate about specific details. Wells also said, "We do not have a car, we do not have the children, we do not have the suspect."

The Saturday, October 29, 1994 edition of the *Union Daily Times* published a story about the discrepancies in Susan's story. The story described how Mitchell Sinclair had not been expecting Susan on the night of the carjacking that no one had seen her or her children at Wal-Mart, and that Susan had told investigators that she had been driving around aimlessly in the hours before the carjacking. In many ways, the front-page story echoed the doubts many in the community were harboring but hesitated to express. Susan seemed reluctant to speak publicly in order to raise awareness of her missing children and this caused additional speculation that Susan was somehow involved in the disappearance of her children.

There was another issue surrounding the disappearance of Michael and Alex Smith that caused a greater amount of speculation, the fact that Susan claimed that the carjacker was a black man. Many in the black community found that Susan's story lacked credibility. They found it impossible that a black man would go unnoticed driving around with two white children, especially given the intensity surrounding the search for the Smith children.

The news media continued to descend on Union. Among the media that was attracted to the case was the television program *American Journal*. The producers of *American Journal* asked Marc Klaas, the father of Polly Klaas, the twelve year old girl from Petaluma, California who was kidnapped from her bedroom and murdered in 1993, to report on the Smith brothers disappearance. Klaas had previously reported on three other cases of missing children for the television program. After his daughters murder, Klaas became an advocate for children, giving up the ownership of a Hertz Rent-A-Car franchise at the San Francisco airport in order to devote his full attention to his new role. A year after becoming a board member of the Polly Klaas Foundation, Klaas formed his own organization, The Marc Klaas Foundation for Children which lobbied for stronger laws to protect children and keep violent, repeat offenders behind bars. Klaas also assists parents who are suffering through the disappearance of a child. When his daughter was kidnapped, Marc Klaas met Jeanne Boyton, a cognitive graphic artist, who sketched the drawing of Richard Allen Davis, the man ultimately caught, tried and convicted for the murder of Polly Klaas. After Polly's murder had been solved, Marc and Jeanne had stayed in touch with each other. When Jeanne saw the drawing of the black man Susan had described to Roy Paschal, she felt that if Susan Smith had really been carjacked, a far more detailed drawing of the suspect would have been produced. Klaas suggested that Jeanne join him in Union. Before Jeanne agreed to go to Union, she called the FBI office in Columbia, South Carolina and obtained their approval. Klaas and Boyton arrived in Union on Friday, October 28, 1994. They had both traveled from the West Coast on red eye flights. As Boyton and Klaas approached the Russell home where Susan was staying, Margaret Gregory met them on the driveway. Gregory is the wife of Susan's cousin and was employed by the Richland County Sheriffs public information office. Bev and Linda Russell had decided that Margaret Gregory would be the official family spokesperson since she was the only member of the extended Russell and Smith families that regularly dealt with the media. Gregory told Klaas and Boyton that Susan had no interest in meeting with them. Jeanne could not understand why Susan wouldn't meet with them. Jeanne had worked on over 7,000 criminal cases and she felt she understood what type of behavior was typical and what wasn't and Susan's refusal to see them was atypical.

Klaas stayed with the media camped out in front of the Russell home while Boyton went to the sheriff's office in Union. Boyton meet with FBI agents, SLED investigators and Union County sheriff's deputies and explained her criticism of the original drawing of the carjacker. Boyton explained how the positioning in the drawing was incorrect, how the suspect was devoid of emotion and how the drawing was of a person that was very passive. Boyton learned from the SLED investigators, the FBI agents and Sheriff Wells that they did not believe Susan Smith. Boyton tried to meet with Susan on her own. She changed from her black business suit into jeans and a casual shirt. She tucked her long blond hair into a baseball cap, but when she approached the Russell home, Margaret Gregory met her in the driveway and again told her that Susan was not interested in meeting with her.

Klaas had spoken briefly to Bev Russell and Margaret Frierson on Friday, his first day in Union, but he was unsuccessful in setting up a meeting with Susan or David Smith. Klaas eventually spoke to David's father who was supportive of the idea of Klaas meeting with David and Susan. Klaas and David's father tentatively set an appointment for Sunday morning but when Klaas arrived at the Russell home to meet with Susan and David, he was met again by Margaret Gregory who told him that Susan and David were not up for meeting him.

After four days of trying to talk to Susan and David Smith, Boyton and Klaas gave up and went home. Marc Klaas left Union convinced that Susan Smith was involved in the disappearance of her children. Klaas did not believe that Susan harmed her children; instead he thought that the Smiths were involved in a custody battle and that Susan had hidden the children from David.

Six days after the Smith children disappeared, the Union County sheriff's office received a call from police in Seattle about a fourteen-month-old white child. The child's description matched the physical description of Alex Smith. The child had been abandoned by a man driving a car with South Carolina license plates at a motel near Seattle. Sheriff Wells called the Russell home and spoke to Bev and told him about the boy in Seattle. For a short period of time, it looked like one of the Smith children had been located. Unfortunately, the good news was short lived. By 10:00 a.m., a call from the police in Seattle confirmed that the boy was not Alex Smith. Sheriff Wells meet with Bev, Linda, David, Susan, and Margaret Gregory, her husband and Scotty and Wendy Vaughn in his office. Wells told them about the disappointing news. After their meeting with Wells, David and Susan held a short press conference in front of the Union County sheriff's office.

Sheriff Wells, Robert Stewart, the Chief of SLED, Agent David Caldwell, the behavioral specialist and the FBI Agents working on the case had each concluded on their own and together as a group that Susan Smith was lying about her involvement in the disappearance of her children. The investigators now faced the challenge of proving Susan's involvement in the crime. Investigators continued to interview Susan on a daily basis. Gradually they began to suggest to her that while they wanted to believe her story, they could not.

Agent Caldwell had accused Susan of murdering her children during an interview on October 26th. Susan's reaction shocked the investigators. The quiet, passive, semi-hysterical woman who continually repeated, "God, look after my babies," suddenly became angry and lashed out at the investigators. From Susan's response, investigators learned that Susan was not just a brokenhearted mother but a strong willed woman and that they would have a difficult time getting her to confess. There was nothing that the investigators could prove yet, but all the details of Susan's story: the red light at the Monarch Mills intersection; the absence of cars on the road; the conflicting stories about where Susan was headed the night of October 25, and the fact that Susan's car had vanished, made investigators doubt her. The issue that most nagged at the investigators was Susan's car. Very early in the investigation, investigators felt that Susan was culpable of the crime and that she had acted alone, but where was Susan's car? Investigators felt that the car and the children were within walking distance of the lake. They returned time again to search for the car in the two-mile area surrounding the McClouds' house.

From the start of the case, investigators carried out meticulously planned interrogations of Susan Smith that were designed to gradually break down her defenses so that she would confess. The investigators behavior and movements were carefully scripted and choreographed. There were no ad libbed or casual questions to Susan. Sheriff Wells and Agent Pete Logan acted as the "good cops." Logan has thirty-five years of law enforcement experience; twenty-seven of those years were spent in the FBI. Logan spoke gently to Susan and manipulated her into trusting him. The investigators believed that if they could build Susan's trust in them, they could coax her into confessing. Logan was careful not to push Susan too hard.

Investigators were familiar with Susan's previous suicide attempts and they were concerned that if they pushed her too hard she would shut down or commit suicide.

The investigators all hoped that the Smith children would be found alive and unharmed, but they knew as the days passed that this wish was less and less likely to come true. The strongest weapon that investigators were able to use against Susan's steadfast claim that she was the victim of a carjacking was psychology. Investigators met several times each day during the nine days that the Smith children were missing to plot strategy and consider their next move in interrogating Susan.

Investigators met with Susan at two different locations away from the news media. Agent Pete Logan met daily with Susan and after each conversation, Logan would attach Susan to the polygraph machine and test her. Susan routinely failed the question: "Do you know where your children are?"

After Agent Caldwell interviewed Susan and studied her behavior, he wrote a psychological profile of her. Caldwell's profile described a cool, cunning woman with a strong drive to succeed. Agent Caldwell had obtained information from Tom Findlay, whom had met with investigators at the beginning of the investigation. Findlay had provided the investigators with a copy of the letter that he had sent to Susan ending their relationship. Findlay told the investigators that Susan had reacted vindictively to his rejection and Findlay had been surprised by Susan's bitterness. The investigators used Findlay's information and their own observations of Susan's angry outburst when confronted with their early suspicions to develop a possible motive: that greed and ambition had pushed Susan to rid herself of her children by murdering them. Agent Caldwell

designed a series of questions and comments for Pete
Logan to use in his length daily conversations with Susan.
Several of the scenarios would be used to during the nine-
day interrogations as part of Logan's efforts to pressure
Susan into confessing.

One of the investigators tactics was to build up the media
frenzy directed at David and Susan Smith. One example of
the way the investigators shaped the news was at the press
conference held by Sheriff Wells on Tuesday, November 1,
exactly one week after Susan made her claims about being
carjacked. Wells met in the parking lot of the Union
County courthouse with a dozen reporters. Wells words
were carefully scripted and impeccably planned. There was
no question to which Wells statement was directed to:
Susan Smith. Wells said, "I don't know that were any
closer to finding the car." "I have nothing encouraging."
"Were following old information that we've just not gotten
to. "I don't think it's developed into anything as of yet to
be any more excited about than yesterday."

The investigators contacted the producers of *Americas
Most Wanted* and had them tape a segment on the
disappearance of the Smith brothers. The investigators
hoped that the additional media coverage would bring
pressure on Susan and would push her to confess. The
investigators contacted a group of Unions most influential
ministers to arrange for them to hold a press conference to
appeal to the carjacker. Agent Caldwell's most elaborate
scheme involved the creation of an authentic appearing
newspaper on desktop publishing software that contained
an article about a young mother who had killed her
children, then served a short prison sentence and upon her
release from prison, married a wealthy physician. A
photograph of a policewoman Susan did not know would
be used. Caldwell's intention was to convince Susan to

confess with the expectation that she might lead a different life with a wealthy man.

The *Americas Most Wanted* segment never aired, the newspaper was never created and the ministers gathered in front of the cameras in front of the Union County courthouse, not to appeal to the carjacker, but to ask for understanding.

The Confession

On Thursday, November 3, 1994, the ninth day since the
carjacking and disappearance of the Michael and Alex
Smith, their parents, Susan and David rose early to prepare
themselves for interviews on three television network
morning programs. Susan and David sat together holding
hands on the Russell's living room sofa during their
interviews. On *CBS This Morning*, Susan was asked if she
had any involvement in her sons disappearance. Susan
answered the question by saying, "I did not have anything
to do with the abduction of my children." Susan added that,
"Whoever did this is a sick and emotionally unstable
person." Although David and Susan were legally separated,
when David was asked whether he believed his wife, he
replied, "Yes, I believe my wife totally."

After the interviews, Susan and David had been scheduled
to sit for an interview with the *Union Daily Times*, but
Margaret Gregory called and cancelled the interview
explaining that the couple were exhausted and had enough
media attention for the day.

At 12:30 p.m., Susan told her mother that she and David
were going to run errands. Susan did not tell her mother
that Sheriff Wells had sent for her. Susan was taken to
another safe house for another interrogation.

Susan was dressed in jeans and a hooded sweatshirt and
brought to her latest interrogation a newly revised
statement that said the same things as her previous
statement, the only change being that the name "Monarch
Mills" had been changed to "Carlisle". Agent Logan asked
Susan if she had anything else to add to her statement and

she said no. At that point, Sheriff Wells was summoned to speak with Susan.

Susan was beginning to be worn down by the intensive and lengthy interrogations. Susan had also been facing increasingly skeptical news reporters who had started to pressure her for an explanation of Sheriff Wells' statement regarding the unspecified inconsistencies in her story.

At 1:40 p.m., Sheriff Wells and Susan met in a small room in the Family Center of the First Baptist Church, located on the same street as the Union County Courthouse. Sheriff Wells and Susan sat on folding chairs, knee to knee, facing one another and talked.

Sheriff Wells confronted Susan about her story of the carjacking. Wells told Susan that he knew that Susan's story of the black carjacker was a lie. He told her that she could not stop at the red light at the Monarch intersection if there were no other cars on the road. Wells told Susan that she had revised her statement because of this inconsistency and that even her back up story was a lie. Wells told Susan that he had undercover officers at the Carlisle intersection working on a drug investigation and that they did not see the alleged carjacker. Wells told Susan that he would have to tell the news media that her story about the alleged black carjacker was not true because Susan's accusation had caused tension in Unions black community. After Wells told Susan this, she asked him to pray with her. At the close of the prayers Wells said, "Lord, we know that all things will be revealed to us in time." Wells then looked at Susan and said, "Susan, it is time."

Susan dropped her head and wailed, "I am so ashamed, I am so ashamed." She asked Sheriff Wells for his gun so that she could kill herself. Sheriff Wells asked Susan why she wanted to do that and Susan replied, "You don't understand, my children are not all right."

Susan told Wells about the crushing isolation she had felt while driving her Mazda along Highway 49 on the night of October 25th and the consuming desire she had to commit suicide. Susan had planned to drive her sons to her mother's house, but emotionally she felt so bad that she felt even her mother could not help her. Susan told Wells that her whole life had felt wrong and that she felt she could not escape the loneliness, isolation and failure that had ensnared her. Susan told Wells about her abortion, her troubled marriage to David and her affair with Tom Findlay.

Susan, teary-eyed

Susan collapsed and began to sob; other investigators entered the room to obtain her written confession. In her confession, Susan filled two pages with carefully written script, rounding off her letters and drawing little hearts whenever she wanted to use the word heart. Susan wrote that she had driven off Highway 49 and onto the road leading to John D. Long Lake because she wanted to commit suicide. She believed that her children would be better off with her and with God than if they were left without a mother and alone. Her plan was that the three of them: Susan, Michael and Alex would die together.

Susan told the investigators that she had tried to end all of their lives by putting the car in neutral and letting it roll down the boat ramp, but she pulled on the parking brake and stopped the car. She did this three times before she stood outside the car and overcome with grief, loneliness and pain reached into the car and released the parking brake sending the car into John D. Long Lake.

It is interesting to note that according to a National Center for Missing and Exploited Children study of murdered children in the United States, completed in the mid-1990s, mothers who murdered their children disposed of their bodies in a distinctively womb-like manner. The study found that some victims were submerged in water and others were found carefully wrapped in plastic. Furthermore, the study also described how all the victims' bodies were found within ten miles of their family home.

During her confession, Susan told investigators how much she loved her sons and that she never meant to harm them and that she was sorry. After the car had rolled into the lake, Susan wanted to undo what she had done, but she could not. As she ran towards the McCloud's house, Susan planned her alibi.

Susan told investigators that keeping her secret during the nine days her sons were assumed to be kidnapped was very difficult. She said that watching her parents and David and his parents hurt her very deeply. Susan said she was scared, but admitted that she thought she would be found out and that her story would not withstand scrutiny.

After nine days of theories, speculations and unanswered questions, Sheriff Wells was left with the task of confirming the answers Susan provided to Michael and Alex's disappearance in her confession. Sheriff Wells wanted to confirm the contents of Susan's confession before breaking the news to David, the Smith family and Susan's family. Sheriff Wells sent for a team of divers from the South Carolina Department of Natural Resources and SLED agents to secure and search John D. Long Lake for Susan's car. Sheriff Wells wanted to tell the families about Susan's confession in person as soon as confirmation that the Mazda and Michael and Alex were resting on the bottom of John D. Long Lake was obtained.

The first divers to arrive at John D. Long Lake were Curtis Jackson and Mike Gault. They paddled out in a small boat onto the lake and Jackson dove into the water. His first dive yielded no results. Gault told Jackson some of the details that Susan Smith had revealed during her interrogation that Gault had learned from Sheriff Wells. Six minutes into his second dive, Jackson located the underside of the upside down Mazda; however his divers light failed and he was unable to see into the car. The next divers to arrive, Steve Morrow and Francis Mitchum, were equipped with more sophisticated diving lights. Morrow and Mitchum located the Mazda in approximately eighteen feet of water. At the place in the lake where the car was located, visibility was only twelve inches.

Morrow and Mitchum made a slow search around the Mazda Protégé and observed that all of the windows were rolled up and that all four doors were closed. Morrow later testified at Susan's trial that he saw a small hand against the window glass. Morrow also testified that we had to be down on the bottom of the lake to see inside the car...they were in car seats hanging upside down. Morrow added that, I was able to determine one occupant on either side of the vehicle. Morrow and Mitchum reported their observations to Sheriff Wells. Sheriff Wells flew from the lake, in a waiting SLED helicopter, to the Russell home to inform David Smith and Susan's parents that Michael and Alex had been found. Unfortunately, the family had already heard an unconfirmed Associated Press report that Susan had confessed to murdering her children. Sheriff Wells stayed at the Russell home for about 20 minutes. Wells told the family members and friends assembled at the home portions of what Susan had told him during her confession and confirmed Susan's account of rolling the Mazda with Michael and Alex strapped inside the car into the lake. Wells also told them that Susan had been arrested and charged with two counts of murder. A bail hearing would be arranged the following day at the Union County Courthouse.

Sheriff Howard Wells (right)
announces Susan's arrest

Immediately after her arrest, strong hatred was directed at
Susan. Shouts of baby killer! And Murderer! Greeted Susan
as she was led from the sheriff's office to a waiting car to
be driven to the York County Jail.

Sheriff Wells held a press conference at 5:00 p.m. to
announce that Susan had confessed and had been arrested
and charged with two counts of murder in connection with
the deaths of her sons, Michael and Alex and that divers
had located her car with two bodies inside. Wells would not
answer questions about the motive, but the news media
speculated on the letter Tom Findlay wrote to Susan that
stated he did not want a readymade family.

The press conference attracted many residents of Union.
Some in the crowd were angered that until Susan Smith's
story was confirmed, the made-up story of a black carjacker
was believed.

John D. Long Lake

Susan's 1990 Mazda, after it was pulled from the lake

After his press conference, Sheriff Wells returned to John
D. Long Lake to be on the scene when the Mazda was
pulled from the water. It took about forty-five minutes to

pull the car through the mud along the lake bottom and into shallow water. Once the car was in shallow water, it was flipped right side up. The windshield of the car had cracked from the temperature changes and water pressure at the bottom of the lake.

The bodies of Michael and Alex were placed in a waiting ambulance that was then driven to the University of South Carolina Medical Center in Charleston. Autopsies were performed on Friday, November 4th and confirmed that the children had been alive when their mother sent them in her car into the lake and that they had drowned as the car submerged.

In the days immediately after Susan Smith confessed there were many newspaper editorials condemning those who were quick to believe blacks were responsible for the carjacking as well as for many of society's problems. In some of the editorials, the Smith case was compared to the 1989 case of Charles Stuart. Stuart was a Boston man who shot and killed his pregnant wife in a parked car and then called 911 to report that he and his wife had been attacked by a black man. Stuarts 911 call was broadcast repeatedly in the days after the crime took place. Stuart claimed that the black man robbed Stuart and his wife of their wallets and jewelry and then shot Mrs. Stuart in the head and Stuart in the stomach. During their investigation, the Boston police aggressively questioned a large number of black men in the Roxbury neighborhood of Boston. Roxbury has a large African American population. Gradually, investigators became suspicious of Stuart and his story. Stuart, fearing that the truth was about to emerge, committed suicide by jumping off a bridge. Boston's African American community was outraged by the treatment that the young men in their community had received during the Stuart investigation and leaders staged rallies and demanded the resignation of several policemen and an apology from city officials.

Fortunately Union was different than Boston. The towns black ministers preached messages of healing, rather than division. On Friday, November 4, the night after Susan confessed, the people of Union held a town meeting to pledge their desire for unity in the face of the Smith tragedy.

More than one hundred blacks and whites attended the meeting hoping to find comfort as well as send a message to the nation that Union was not bitterly divided along racial lines. One of the black ministers, Reverend A.J. Brackett, the pastor of St. Paul Baptist Church, pointed out that only a few black men had been stopped by investigators during their search for the alleged carjacker and that only two black men had been brought to the sheriff's office for questioning. Both men were treated courteously and released after a short time.

On Friday, November 4, the day after Susan Smith confessed, her brother, Scotty Vaughn, apologized to the black community of Union by reading a letter to the news media. In his letter, Vaughn said, we apologize to all of the black citizens of Union and everywhere and hope you won't believe any of the rumors that this was ever a racial issue.

The night that Susan was arrested, she wrote David a letter. The letter was filled with the phrase, I'm sorry, and complaints that Susan's feelings were getting lost in the midst of everyone else's sorrow. David was upset by the contents of the letter and thought, what kind of person is Susan? David had the same thoughts after he read Susan's confession.

The funeral for Michael and Alex was held on Sunday, November 6th at Buffalo Methodist Church. The funeral was preceded by a visitation on Saturday, November 5th. The casket remained closed during the visitation and funeral because of the water damage done to the bodies. Michael and Alex were buried together in a white casket with gold trim during a private ceremony in the cemetery behind the Bogansville United Methodist Church, next to the grave of Danny Smith, David's older brother and the children's uncle.

The funeral for Michael and Alex was held on Sunday, November 6th at Buffalo Methodist Church. The funeral was preceded by a visitation on Saturday, November 5th. The casket remained closed during the visitation and funeral because of the water damage done to the bodies. Michael and Alex were buried together in a white casket with gold trim during a private ceremony in the cemetery behind the Bogansville United Methodist Church, next to the grave of Danny Smith, David's older brother and the children's uncle.

The boys' coffin

Michael and Alexander's Grave site

Memorial at John D. Long Lake

The Trial

After Susan was arrested for the murders of Michael and
Alex, she was held without bail at the York County Jail. On
the evening that Susan was arrested, Bev and Linda Russell
hired David Bruck, a Columbia, South Carolina attorney
specializing in death penalty cases, to represent Susan. The
Russell's would eventually be forced to mortgage their
home in order to pay for Bruck's services.

David Bruck

Bruck was 46 when agreed to represent Susan Smith. He
had attended Harvard College and graduated *magna cum
laude*. After college, Bruck attended the University of
South Carolina Law School and graduated in 1975. Before
beginning his law practice, Bruck traveled throughout
United States and Canada, eventually returning to South
Carolina to represent clients facing the death penalty
because he was convinced that these defendants did not
receive adequate legal representation. Bruck was also
disturbed by the fact that the death penalty population in

South Carolina was made up largely of poor black men. Prior to defending Susan Smith, Bruck had represented 50 people charged with capital murder before juries or at the appellate level. Of Bruck's 50 capital clients, he has only lost three to death sentences. He has saved many of his clients from death sentences by winning new trials that have resulted in life sentences and in one case, an acquittal. Other defense attorneys praise Bruck for being shrewd and for being able to localize his intelligence. One admirer said Bruck can be chameleon-like, he understands that arguing a case in Columbia, South Carolina is different than arguing a case in Union.

Judy Clarke

David Bruck hired Judith Clarke, an attorney who is an expert in death penalty cases, to assist him with Susan's trial. Judy Clarke is a federal public defender from Washington State who took a leave of absence from her job to work on Susan Smith's defense. In 1997, Clarke would work on the defense of the Unabomber, Theodore Kaczynski, helping to set up a plea that would spare Kaczynski from being sentenced to death.

The prosecutor for Susan Smith's trial was Union County Solicitor Thomas Pope, 32, who, at the time of the Smith trial, was the youngest prosecutor in the state of South Carolina. Pope grew up in Union and attended the University of South Carolina for college and law school. Before joining the Solicitors office, Pope worked as an undercover drug agent for the State Law Enforcement Division. Pope is the son of a South Carolina sheriff and had tried one other murder case before the Smith case, the case of a father who confessed to smothering his son. In that case, Pope accepted a plea bargain of an eight-year prison sentence for the father. Pope was considered young, articulate and hardworking.

Thomas Pope

On Friday, November 5, a three-minute hearing was held before Judge Larry Patterson. Susan was not present because she had waived her right to be present at the hearing and her right to bail. David Bruck was present at the hearing, after having met with Susan for the first time at the York County Jail.

On November 18, 1994, a hearing was held before Circuit Judge John Hayes at the request of Solicitor Thomas Pope. Pope requested that Susan undergo a psychological examination by an impartial physician to determine whether she was criminally responsible for the crime she had confessed to and if she was competent to stand trial. David Bruck objected to the evaluation stating that the information contained in it could later be used against Susan if Pope chose to seek the death penalty. Judge Hayes put off ruling on the request and asked Pope to submit for his review a list of cases where judges ordered psychiatric evaluations of defendants. One week later, Pope filed a fifty-eight page brief. In late November, Judge Hayes ruled against the State, stating that the request for a neutral examination was premature, given that David Bruck had not yet said whether Susan would be offering an insanity defense at her trial.

From the time after her bail hearing until her trial, Susan was jailed at the Women's Correctional Facility in Columbia, 70 miles south of Union. She was given both physical and psychological evaluations by the prison staff and placed on a twenty-four-hour suicide watch. Susan was checked every fifteen minutes by a prison guard. This suicide watch continued for eight months until Susan's trial began. Susan was housed in a six-by-fourteen-foot cell where a light was on twenty-four hours a day so that a closed circuit television camera could monitor her. Susan was allowed to keep a bible, a blanket, and her glasses in her cell. She was also allowed short visits from her family. Because she was on a suicide watch, Susan wore a paper gown.

About three weeks after Susan had confessed, she asked David to visit her at the Women's Correctional Facility. David and Susan met for one hour. Susan apologized again and again for killing their sons, but when David asked her why she had committed the crime; Susan did not have an answer. David left feeling sorry for Susan, although his feeling later changed and he became angry with her.

David Smith

David Smith learned some terrible details of the crime during the time leading up to Susans trial. One of those things David learned was that Susan seemed to have known exactly where her car had sunk in John D. Long Lake. Divers had searched the lake twice during their nine-day investigation, once on Thursday, October 27th and again on Sunday, October 30, but did not find the car.

David learned that when Susan confessed, she told investigators exactly where to find her car. David was left to draw one conclusion: that Susan waited to see her sons die. David also learned that when the car was dragged from the lake and flipped over, the lights came on. David believed that Susan intentionally left the lights on so that she could watch the car sink out of sight. David came to believe that Susan was desperate to win Tom Findlay back and terrified that her affair with J. Carey Findlay would be revealed. David believed that Susan would do anything and he believed that the murders were premeditated.

On January 16, 1995, Solicitor Thomas Pope filed a notice of intention to seek the death penalty against Susan Smith. The notice stated that the State of South Carolina would offer evidence at Susan's trial that two aggravating circumstances existed in the murders of Michael and Alex Smith. The two circumstances that made Susan Smith eligible for the death penalty were the fact that she murdered two people during one act and that the murders were committed against children under the age of eleven.

On January 27, 1995, Judge William Howard issued a gag order prohibiting the prosecutors, defense attorneys and investigators from releasing any prejudicial information that had not been presented to the court. Prior to the beginning of the trial, Judge Howard would rule in favor of a defense motion to ban television cameras from the courtroom during the trial. Judge Howard based his ruling on what he considered to be the circus like atmosphere that television cameras had created in the O.J. Simpson trial that was ongoing in Los Angeles as well as the pre-trial publicly the case had received. Judge Howard also wanted to keep a tight rein on the length of the trial as well as the conduct of the trial participants.

In February, the defense hired a team of psychiatrists led by Dr. Seymour Halleck to conduct a psychiatric evaluation of Susan at the Women's Correctional Facility. Halleck interviewed Susan for 15 hours over four sessions in February, March and June.

Halleck diagnosed Susan as having a "dependent personality disorder" and described her as a person who "feels she can't do things on her own." "She constantly needs affection and becomes terrified that she'll be left alone." Halleck found that Susan was only depressed when she was alone. She almost always was in a normal mood when she was around people. In Halleck's opinion, Susan did not suffer from deep depression. Halleck found that Susan became suicidal when she was depressed. Halleck also studied Susan's family history and concluded based on her family history and his psychiatric interviews with her that Susan had a tendency toward depression that began in her childhood. Halleck believed that Susan's family tree had a genetic predisposition for depression because so many of her relatives had symptoms of depression and alcoholism.

Bev and Linda Russell separated in February and Bev moved in with his aunt, while Linda lived in their Mount Vernon Estates home. Bev resigned from the state Republican executive committee, explaining that for personal reasons, he could no longer serve.

On March 23, 1995, Judge Howard ordered Susan to undergo an evaluation by Dr. Donald Morgan, a psychiatrist from the University of South Carolina. Dr. Morgan's evaluation was conducted on behalf of the prosecution.

Susan and David's divorce became final in May. At a brief hearing, that Susan waived her right to attend, Tom Findlay testified about their adultery. In the final divorce settlement, David and Susan divided Michael and Alex's toys and clothing in half. David received the Mazda that he later had destroyed after Susan's trial was completed.

In June, Susan received a letter from Bev Russell. Russell wrote, "My heart breaks for what I have done to you." Russell also wrote that, "I want you to know that you do not have all the guilt for this tragedy." The letter was dated June 18, 1995, Father's day.

Before Susan's trial began on July 10, 1995, there was speculation about the arguments her attorneys would use in her defense during her trial. Many expected Susan's attorneys to argue that she was the victim of destructive relationships and influences since her birth. The prosecution was expected to paint Susan as a scheming monster who lied to her family, friends, hometown and the nation for nine days when she blamed a phantom black carjacker for the disappearance of her two sons, before confessing that she had drown her children.

Along with the speculation of what type of defense Susan would argue at her trial, there was speculation about Susan and Susan's personality. To many people in Union, it appeared that during Susan's 23 years she had developed a dual personality, she presented one side of her personality to some and the other side of her personality to others. One side of Susan's personality was described as manipulative and deceitful and capable of ending her children's lives in order to improve her own. Was it was possible that this side of Susan's personality murdered her children in the hope of reclaiming her boyfriend, Tom Findlay? Or was Susan suffering from a psychiatric condition that explained why her behavior caused the death of her children? Many people hoped that these questions would answer the question of why Susan had murdered her children.

Prior to the start of the trial, Bruck proposed that Susan plead guilty to the murders of her children and be sentenced to 30 years to life in prison, without the possibility of parole, but this plea bargain was rejected by Thomas Pope. Pope said that he sought the death penalty "after careful deliberation and consultation with family members of the victims." Pope also said that he sought the death penalty based on the facts of the case.

In a move that some questioned at the time that it was made, David Bruck did not request a change in venue from Union to another town. In retrospect, this was a very shrewd maneuver. Bruck was convinced that if he could gain the sympathy of Susan's hometown, her neighbors and residents of the community where she grew up, he could spare her life. Bruck had correctly noted that the mood of the black and white residents of Union had softened and that Susan had become the object of prayer vigils. Bruck found that more Union residents were willing to accept that Susan was mentally ill, than thought she was evil. Bruck believed that jurors from Susan's hometown would have a difficult time sentencing her to death.

A few days before the start of her trial and with the permission of David Bruck, Susan's pastor, Mark Long, held a press conference to reveal that Susan had undergone a jailhouse Christian conversion and baptism.

There was some speculation regarding the timing of Susan's conversion. Some people expressed the feeling that it seemed too convenient and useful to Susan because of her upcoming trial.

On July 11, 1995, after a two-day hearing, Judge Howard ruled that Susan was mentally competent to stand trial. This ruling was made even though the states psychiatrist, Dr. Donald Morgan, who had testified at the competence hearing, stated that he believed that Susan might try to sabotage her own defense, if she took the witness stand, because she wanted to die. Morgan had examined Susan in April, May and June for approximately ten hours and diagnosed Susan as manifesting an "adjustment disorder with mixed emotional features, including some depression." Although Susan appeared listless during the court session and was dependent upon Prozac, an anti-depressant drug to help her understand and follow the proceedings, Judge Howard ruled that the trial could proceed.

The trial was held at the Union County Courthouse, which was originally designed by Robert Mills, who also designed the Washington Monument. The courthouse was rebuilt between 1911 and 1913 and renovated in 1974. Judge William Howard's courtroom on the second floor of the courthouse is one of the largest in South Carolina and contained thirteen rows of benches for members of the press and the public. The first two rows of benches on the left-hand side of the courtroom were reserved for Susan's family and friends and the first two rows of benches on the right hand side of the courtroom were reserved for David Smiths family and friends. During the trial, all the seats were filled and crowds of people were turned away from the proceedings. The courtroom was old and the acoustics were terrible. If the attorneys or witnesses moved from their microphones, it was difficult to hear what was being said. The floor creaked which forced Judge Howard to enforce a strict order prohibiting the public from moving from their seats when court was in session.

The pace of the trial would be fast. Judge Howard set a Monday through Saturday schedule beginning on the trials first day, July 10, 1995.

Jury selection moved quickly and was completed on the sixth day of the trial, July 16, 1995. Lawyers interviewed 55 prospective jurors out of 250 people called during the jury selection process. Many of those interviewed said that they were strongly opposed to the death penalty. The jury was composed of 12 jurors and two alternates and was a mix of blue-collar workers, merchants and professionals. The 12 jurors were composed of seven whites and five blacks. Almost all of the white jurors, five men and two women, had friends or acquaintances on the list of witnesses for the trial, but they said they could put aside their feelings and friendships and decide the case based on the evidence presented. The black jurors, four men and one woman, did not seem to be acquainted with Susan, her friends, family or people listed as witnesses for the trial.

Judge William Howard

Originally, Judge William Howard had wanted six alternates, but after meeting with both the prosecution and defense attorneys, it was agreed that jury selection would be complete with just two alternates.

At one point, after the jury was selected, Bruck argued that the jury was biased because of the 12 jurors, nine were men and only three were women. Bruck argued that the jury was not representative of the community, but his argument was overruled.

On Tuesday, July 18, 1995, the day the trial was set to begin, the Union County Courthouse received a bomb threat that required the evacuation of everyone inside. The man who telephoned the threat was quickly found and arrested.

Opening statements began on Wednesday, July 19, 1995. Special Prosecutor Keith Giese, assistant to Solicitor Thomas Pope, began his opening statement by stating the facts of the prosecution's case. For nine days in the fall of 1994, Susan Smith looked this country in the eye and lied. She begged God to return her children to safety, and the whole time she knew her children were lying dead at the bottom of John D. Long Lake. Giese continued by telling jurors that Michael and Alex Smith died because their mother thought she could reclaim Tom Findlay, a lover who had discarded her. The stumbling block to Mrs. Smith getting Tom Findlay back was her children. Giese added that, Mrs. Smith removed that obstacle from her life. Toward the end of his statement, Giese told the jurors that, this is a case of selfishness, of I, I, I, and me, me, me. Giese concluded his statement by asking jurors to hold on to their common sense in the weeks ahead, because they would come to see Susan Smith as a selfish, manipulative killer who sacrificed her children for love of the son of a rich industrialist. The prosecution's case was based on the theory that Susan wanted to escape her loneliness, unhappiness and the stresses in her life by establishing an exciting, intimate relationship with her wealthy boyfriend. In order to live this new life; Susan would need to free herself of her children and the demands of motherhood.

The defenses opening statement was given by Judy Clarke, who asked the jurors to look into their hearts, and through that softer focus, find a disturbed, child-like figure who, after a lifetime of sadness, just snapped. Clarke told jurors that Susan was deeply depressed and had a sense of failure in her life. This sense of failure included acts of molestation at the hands of her stepfather, the suicide of her father and her own suicide attempts. All of these events contributed to pushing her to the edge of the lake to kill herself and her children. At the last second, her body willed itself out of the car, and she lived and her toddlers died, Clarke added. Clarke told the jury that When we talk about Susan Smith's life, we are not trying to gain your sympathy, were trying to gain your understanding. Clarke stated that Susan's lie is wrong. It's a shame, but it is a child-like lie, from a damaged person. The defenses strategy was to outline Susan's emotional troubles that caused her to drown her two sons. The defense attorneys believed that by portraying Susan as a person with emotional problems, they could save her from the electric chair. Susan's defense attorneys did not claim she was insane or that a mental illness caused her to murder her sons.

Susan leaving courtroom

Throughout the trial, Susan sat at the defense table quietly reading mail or playing with small objects she held in her hands. Susan had been jailed for eight months and her inactivity during those months appeared in a weight gain. Rather than appear child-like as her defense attorneys were trying to suggest during her trial; Susan appeared older than her 23 years. Her appearance was dowdy. Susan wore plain, conservative suits that aged her. Susan wore wire-rimmed glasses and her face generally had a serene expression, except when there was discussion about her sons, then she would cry, briefly and discreetly.

The first witness to testify at the trial was Shirley McCloud. McCloud testified about Susan's appearance at her front door. McCloud told the jury that when Linda Russell came to be with her daughter, one of the first things that she did was to scold Susan for not locking her car doors.

Among the first witnesses called to testify were the law enforcement agents and investigators who were involved in the case. Sheriff Howard Wells testified how he had tricked Susan into confessing with a small lie of his own.

Wells described how on the afternoon of November 3, 1994, he told Susan that he knew her claim that her children had been taken at an intersection outside of Union was a lie because he had assigned sheriff's deputies to conduct a surveillance at the crossroads. Wells told her that "this could not happen as you said." Wells told the jury that there had been no deputies at the intersection and that, "I told her I would release it to the media because the lie about a black carjacker was causing deep pain among blacks, and he owed it to the town to end the racial divisiveness it had caused." According to Wells, Susan then broke down and confessed to the murders. Wells also testified that even though he was suspicious of Susan, he did not arrest her because he was not certain until she confessed what had happened to Michael and Alex.

After the first day of testimony, Judge Howard removed a juror from the panel and had her jailed. Gayle Beam, the only black woman on the jury, was held in contempt of court and jailed because she did not disclose on her jury questionnaire that she had recently plead guilty to credit card fraud. Beam was questioned by Judge Howard and admitted that she had not looked at the questionnaire that the court required her to complete and instead had her daughter complete it for her. Beam faced a fine of $10,000 and a sentence up to six months in jail, if found guilty of the charges. One of the two alternate jurors was selected and replaced Beam.

On the second day of the trial, Pete Logan, the State Law Enforcement Division agent who spent 24 hours interrogating Susan testified. Logan described Susan's troubled life and her sexual relationships. Logan told the jury that Susan had sex with her estranged husband, David, on October 21, four days before murdering her sons. It was during this encounter that Susan claimed that David told her that he tapped her home telephone and knew about the affair she was having with Carey Findlay, the owner of Conso Products. Logan testified about Susan prior suicide attempts and the remorse that she showed during her confession.

Other investigators followed Logan and testified that from the beginning of the case, they were suspicious of Susan. These witnesses described a woman who cried without shedding any tears, who seemed more interested in how she looked on television than in having her sons returned and who spoke of going to the beach to get away from hounding reporters.

Roy Paschal, who drew the composite sketch of the phantom carjacker, testified that Susan "started off extremely vague," when describing the alleged carjackers physical appearance.

David Espie, the FBI agent who administered several polygraph tests to Susan, testified that Susan "would make sobbing noises, but when I would looked at her eyes, there was no water, there were no tears."

Steve Morrow, a diving expert with the South Carolina Department of National Resources and one of the divers who searched for the missing car, also testified on the second day of the trial. Morrow testified about finding the car with the Smith children inside. Morrow described how along with the bodies of Michael and Alex Smith, the letter from Tom Findlay telling Susan that their relationship was over was also found in Susan's car.

Tom Findlay testified during the second day of the trial. Findlay testified that he had written a letter to Susan telling her that he did not want to be in a relationship that included children.

By having Findlay testify and introducing his letter into evidence, the prosecution sought to portray Susan as so maliciously selfish that she would trade her sons lives for a chance to reclaim Findlay.

During Findlay's cross-examination by David Bruck, Findlay assisted Susan's defense by telling the jury that he thought Susan was a "sweet, loving person" rather than the monster the prosecution was trying to construct. Bruck also scored points with the jury when he asked Findlay about his sexual relationship with Susan. Findlay testified that the "pleasure she got from sex was not physical pleasure." "It was just in being close, being loved." Another area that Findlay may have assisted Susan was when he testified about David Smiths behavior. Findlay testified about an incident that occurred one year before the murders when he had telephoned Susan Smith one day at her home. Apparently David Smith had hidden in a closet and in an apparent fit of jealously, emerged from the closet, snatched the telephone from Susan and told Findlay that he would harm him if he continued to see Susan.

Three of Susan's co-workers from Conso testified that Susan had on separate occasions told them that she wondered how her life would be different if she had not gotten married and had children at a young age.

After two days of testimony, the state rested its case against Susan Smith. The last witness to testify for the prosecution was Dr. Sandra Conradi, the pathologist who performed the autopsies on Michael and Alex Smith. Conradi testified for

15 minutes because David Bruck stipulated to the identity of the Smith brothers and the fact that drowning was the cause of death. Judge Howard refused to allow prosecutors to show the jury horrific pictures of Michael and Alex after they had been under John D. Long Lake for nine days. Judge Howard also refused to allow prosecutors to question Conradi about the decayed nature of the bodies because he felt that the descriptions were so terrible that they would be prejudicial. Conradi testified that she received the bodies of Michael and Alex Smith still strapped to their car seats and that neither child was wearing shoes.

The state's case was expected to last at least two weeks, however, it moved more quickly than expected because Judge Howard prevented the state from presenting its full case against Susan. Judge Howard limited the evidence presented to the jury and David Bruck often stipulated to points in the case rather than forcing Solicitor Pope to prove them.

Because Susan had confessed to the murders of her sons, her attorneys were left with two choices in defending her. The first choice was to have Susan plead not guilty by reason of insanity. This required that Susan's attorneys prove that she was insane at the time of the murders by demonstrating that she could not distinguish between right and wrong, either morally or legally. The second choice was to have Susan plead guilty, but mentally ill. This would require that Susan's attorneys prove that she was mentally incapable of complying with the law at the time of the murders, even if she knew that her actions were wrong. The problem with the first choice was that Susan was not mentally ill. She was depressed and suicidal, but not insane.

A diagnosis of insanity means that an individual is delusional, schizophrenic or psychotic and Susan was none of these.

David Bruck rejected the second choice because it was determined through examinations conducted by Dr. Halleck that Susan was not mentally ill. The only option open was for the defense to plead that Susan was suffering from severe mental depression and that the murders were a failed suicide in which Susan planned to drown herself as well as her sons.

On Thursday, July 20, 1995, the defense began its case. David Bruck recalled Pete Logan, the SLED Agent, and Carol Allison, the FBI agent who had been originally called by the prosecution, because both were so sympathetic to Susan's case when they testified. Bruck questioned both Logan and Allison about Susan's remorse. Thomas Pope tried to counter the agent's testimony by pointing out to the jury that Smith was an accomplished liar who had misled investigators for nine days.

Arlene Andrews, a social worker at the University of South Carolina, testified about a family tree she had constructed of Susan's family that showed a strong history of deep depression among the Vaughn family. Andrews described several attempted and successful suicides by members of Susan's family.

On Friday July 21, 1995, the defenses most important witness, Dr. Seymour Halleck, testified. Dr. Seymour Halleck is a University of North Carolina psychiatrist and law professor who led the team that examined Susan to determine whether she was competent to stand trial.

Halleck testified that Susan suffered from depression and suicidal thoughts in the months leading up to the October 25th murders and that these thoughts allowed her to fall into a destructive cycle of sexual relationships in order to ease her loneliness. Halleck testified that Susan had sex with four different men during the six-week period leading up to the murders. Susan had also begun to drink heavily during this period of time.

Halleck testified that Susan had sex with her stepfather, Beverly Russell; Tom Findlay, her boyfriend at the time; with J. Carey Findlay, the owner of the mill where she worked; and with her estranged husband, David Smith. Halleck said that Susan's sexual relationships temporarily eased her depression, but that her guilt ultimately deepened her depression. Halleck told the jury that "Much of her sexual activity was not for her own satisfaction." Halleck added that, "Susan was more concerned with pleasing others and making sure that they liked her."

Halleck's testimony was an attempt by the defense to poke holes in the prosecution's theory that Susan murdered her children so that she could rekindle her relationship with Tom Findlay. Halleck dismissed the prosecution's theory that Susan murdered her children to reclaim Findlay saying that it was an "absurd idea." He labeled Susan's affair with Findlay as "passing" and added that Susan had, "strong feelings for a lot of different men and that it was very unlikely that Tom Findlay was number one on her list."

Halleck testified that he thought Susan had sex with J. Carey Findlay because she was molested by her stepfather and had a need for love and approval of an older man. Halleck also testified that Susan had told him that when she slept with Beverly Russell, "it made her skin crawl," and that Halleck thought the reasons that Susan did these things was because she sought love and approval.

Solicitor Pope had Halleck admit that most of his information came from Susan and that her constant need for affection was a symptom of "brief, intermittent depressive disorder," in which Susan was able much of the time to make her co-workers and friends believe that she was fine.

Halleck also described Susan's behavior on the night of the murders and said that he believed that she intended to kill herself, but that a "survival instinct" took over and that she blocked out the presence of her two sons at the instant she released the parking brake. Halleck also described how as Susan ran from the edge of the lake to the McCloud's home she began to make up her story of being carjacked by a black man because she was afraid of what others would think of her. Halleck told the jury that if Susan had been treated for depression with Prozac, the murders would never have occurred.

David Bruck asked Halleck the question that everyone wanted to ask, "Why didn't Susan go into the water?" Halleck answered that he could only assume that "when she ran out of her car, that her self-preservation instincts took over, and although up to that moment she fully intended to kill herself, she got frightened."

Several other defense witnesses testified that Susan had been depressed as a child and that she had been suicidal since the age of ten. After four days of testimony, the defense rested its case. David Bruck told the jury that Susan accepted responsibility for what she did, but that her actions were attributable to her depression.

Closing arguments were given on Saturday, July 22, 1995. Solicitor Pope was impassioned when he described the circumstances of Michael and Alex's deaths. "I submit to you that they were in that car, screaming, crying, calling for their father, while the woman who placed them in that car was running up the hill with her hands covering her ears." Pope went back to his theme that the murders were committed so that Susan could reclaim Tom Findlay and have a life with him. "She used the emergency brake handle like a gun, and eliminated her toddlers so that she could have a chance at a life with Tom Findlay, the man she said she loved."

Judy Clarke was less dramatic and used her closing argument to continue to appeal to the jury's sympathy, saying that Susan had never shown anything "except unconditional love for her children." Clarke continued by telling the jury that, "there was no malice in what she did, so it was not murder." Clarke told the jury that "this is not a case about evil, but a case of sadness and despair." Clarke added that, "Susan had choices in her life, but her choices were irrational and her choices were tragic."

In a ruling that surprised and upset the prosecution and the Smith family, Judge Howard ruled in favor of a defense motion to allow the jury to consider a lesser charge of involuntary manslaughter. If the jury had chosen to convict Susan of involuntary manslaughter, she would have faced a sentence of three to ten years in prison.

Before the jury began deliberations, Judge Howard dismissed one juror saying that he had a family tie to the case. The last alternate juror replaced the dismissed juror.

At 7:55 p.m. after deliberating for two and one half-hours, the jury returned a verdict of guilty of two counts of murder.

As the verdict was read, Susan Smith bowed her head in tears and trembled. The jury appeared to have agreed with the prosecutors who argued that Susan knew what she was doing when she released the emergency brake on her car, allowing it to roll into the lake with her sons inside strapped to their car seats. Prosecutors had argued that Susan killed her sons to rekindle her romance with Tom Findlay, a wealthy boyfriend who told her that he did not want children and the jury agreed with that theory.

The verdict came after five days of testimony and was the first stage in the three-stage process of trial, penalty phase and sentencing. The penalty phase would begin on July 24, 1995.

Penalty Phase

The same jury who convicted Susan Smith of murdering her two sons would decide whether she would die in the electric chair or receive a life in prison sentence in the penalty phase. The penalty phase would be similar to the trial, except that the prosecution had more latitude in building its theory that Susan Smith was a cold-blooded murderer who killed her children in the hope of reclaiming her lover.

Keith Gieses opening statement for the prosecution during the penalty phase was similar to his opening statement during the trial. Giese reminded the jury of Susan's "nine days of deceit and nine days of trickery."

In his opening statement, David Bruck told the jury that "the greatest punishment for Susan Smith would be life in prison, not death." This argument is what Dr. Morgan, the states psychiatric expert witness, and other witnesses said she desired during her trial. Bruck reiterated to the jury that Smith was a deeply depressed and fragile person who made serious mistakes in her life to win love.

Solicitor Thomas Pope began the state's case by showing videotapes of Susan Smith lying about the disappearance of her sons. The first videotape was her tearful plea to the phantom carjacker outside the Union County Courthouse on November 2, 1994. The second videotape was composed of segments of three interviews Susan had given to network morning programs on November 3, 1994, the day she confessed to the crimes.

Three witnesses testified during the first day of the penalty phase for the prosecution. Margaret Frierson, the executive director of the South Carolina Adam Walsh Center, testified that Susan seemed unusually calm for a parent dealing with the disappearance of her children. Margaret Gregory, Susan's cousin, testified about the number of times that Susan had appeared on television and perpetuated her lie that a black man had carjacked her and kidnapped her children. The last witness was Eddie Harris, a SLED agent, who testified that when he transported Susan during her interrogations and he was surprised by her calmness and disinterest in finding her children. Harris testified that at one point Susan had asked him how she appeared on television.

On Tuesday, July 25, 1995, the prosecution presented the heart of its case. David Smith testified that "all his hopes, all my dreams, everything that I had planned for the rest of my life, ended," on October 25, 1994. Smith was dressed in a white shirt and plaid Mickey Mouse tie and at times cried uncontrollably when talking about the nine days he spent believing his sons had been abducted by a carjacker. Smith began to cry, along with at least three of the jurors, when he said, "I didn't know what to do." "Everything I had planned on, my life with my kids was gone." Judge Howard called a recess as Smith tried to collect himself. As Susan Smith was escorted away to a holding cell, she called out softly, "I'm sorry David." David Smith did not look at her.

When the hearing resumed, Thomas Pope raised several potentially damaging cross-examination topics, including the amount of money Smith was paid for co-writing a book about his life with Susan Smith.

Smith testified that he was paid $110,000 and that he kept $20,000 of the $110,000 to help him through the trial, since he had taken a leave of absence from his job as the night manager of the Winn Dixie in Union.

After two hours of difficult testimony, Judge Howard called a lunch recess. David Smith appeared to be drained and collapsed into his father's arms after court was recessed.

In a surprising move, David Bruck did not question David Smith. Bruck had little to gain with a tough cross-examination of David Smith after Smith had won the jurors hearts. Bruck later said that his client had asked him not to cross-examine David Smith.

Videotaped re-enactment of car sinking

The prosecution showed the jury two-videotape re-enactments of Susan Smith's burgundy Mazda rolling down the boat ramp and into the water. During the showing of the videotape of the car filling with water, Prosecutor Keith Giese commented that the rear of the car was rising while the front of the car was filling with water and that Michael and Alex would have faced the lakes water before the water engulfed them. The videotape re-enactment of Susan's Mazda submerging into the lake showed that it took a full six minutes for the car to fill with water before it became completely submerged, because the cars doors and windows were closed.

On Wednesday, July 27, 1995 the prosecution showed the jury pictures taken of Michael and Alex after they had been removed from the Mazda. Judge Howard only allowed photographs showing the brothers discolored and decomposing legs and arms. The judge would not allow several photos showing the full effects of the nine-day submersion to be shown to the jury. After the presentation of the photos, the prosecution rested its case and the defense began its case by calling two witnesses.

Arlene Andrews, the University of South Carolina social work professor who had testified during Susan's trial, testified that David and Susan Smith's relationship was extremely strained and that Susan was thrown into a downward spiral that ended in the murders of her children. Andrews testified that Susan's mental health began to deteriorate in August 1994 after the Smiths final attempt at reconciling their marriage failed. Andrews told the jury that when Susan told David that she would seek a divorce in July 1994, the couple agreed to seek an amiable divorce with neither party blaming the other. However, Susan reneged on this agreement and decided to seek a divorce on the grounds of adultery.

David retaliated against Susan and on October 20th, searched Susan's purse and found the letter Tom Findlay had written her dated October 17, 1994. When David confronted Susan, she confessed to having an affair with Findlay's father, J. Carey Findlay, the owner of Conso Products. David threatened Susan by telling her that he would reveal the relationship to Findlay's wife. Susan became distraught and thought she had done something unforgivable. Andrews testified that Susan's suicidal despair set in and she began to think everything about her was bad. Five days after the argument with David, she murdered their sons.

Scotty Vaughn, Susan's brother made a tearful plea for
mercy on behalf of his sister. We've been devastated
already with the loss of Michael and Alex; it seems sad and
ironic that the tragedy of their loss is going to be used to
sentence Susan to death. Vaughn further testified that
Susan's pain is in living, not in the fear of dying. He added,
I don't think the state could punish her anymore that she's
been punished.

On the last day of the penalty phase, July 27, 1995, Beverly
Russell testified and accepted part of the blame for the
deaths of Michael and Alex Smith. Russell admitted that he
molested Susan when she was a teenager and had
consensual sex with her as an adult. During his testimony,
Russell also told the jury that his sexual relationship with
Susan occurred mostly at his home, only once at Susan and
David's home and once at a motel in Spartenburg. Russell
read from his Father's day letter to Susan. Russell pleaded
for Susan's life, telling the jury that Susan was sick and
even though she loved her children, what happened was
from a sickness...It's horrible.

Thomas Pope gave the prosecutions closing argument.
Pope urged the jury to vote for a death sentence. He told
the jury that there was one theme in the case and it was the
choice that Susan made. Pope reminded the jury that Susan
Smith chose to drive to the lake. Pope continued, she chose
to send Michael and Alex down that ramp. Pope added,
then as heinous as that act was, she carried it even further
by choosing to lie. Pope tried to show the jury that Susan
was fooling them with her claims of remorse, the way she
fooled everyone during the nine-day investigation. Pope
reiterated the prosecution's theory that Susan was selfish
and manipulative and killed her children so that she could
reclaim her boyfriend, Tom Findlay.

In his closing statement, David Bruck took the jury through Susan's family history and life experiences. He explained how the choices Susan made were tragic and how the jury was left with a choice, but that the jury's judgment was more sound than Susan's and that the choice the jury should make was to sentence Susan to life in prison. Toward the end of his closing argument, David Bruck held a bible and read from the Gospel of John about the woman who committed adultery and was to be stoned. He that is without sin among you, let him cast the first stone, Bruck read. Bruck told the jury that Susan's choice to go to the lake will haunt her for the rest of her life.

After the closing arguments were completed, Judge Howard gave Susan one last chance to address the jury, but she declined.

At 4:38 p.m. the jury returned with a unanimous decision after deliberating for two and one half-hours.

The jury rejected the prosecution's request for a sentence of death for Susan and decided instead that Susan should spend the rest of her natural life in prison. The jury had taken the same amount of time to convict Susan as it did to reject the death penalty

At 4:45 p.m., Judge Howard sentenced Susan Smith to thirty years to life in prison. Susan will be eligible for parole in 2025, after she has served 30 years in prison. At that time, Susan will be 53 years old.

Union County Courthouse as news crews wait for sentence

Later when jurors were asked about their decision, they acknowledged that they knew of Sheriff Wells comments after Susan's arrest. Wells had said that if Susan Smith had not confessed, investigators would probably not have been able to amass enough evidence to charge her with the crimes she committed. Jurors saw that Susan had an opportunity to escape punishment, yet she chose not to do so. The jury recognized this fact and considered it a reason to spare her life. Jurors also said that they felt that Susan needed help and did not deserve to be sentenced to death. Jurors believed Susan's attorneys claims that Susan murdered her children while trying to end her own life. Jurors also felt sorry for Susan because of her mental state during the commission of the crimes. Jurors admitted that the closeness of the Union community weighed into their decision to spare Susan's life.

David Smith felt that justice was not served because Susan was not sentenced to death. He said that he respected the jury's decision and the verdict, but did not agree with it. David also said that he would appear at Susan's parole hearings each time she might be considered for release to make sure that her life sentence means life.

The sad facts of the Susan Smith case are these: a young woman, with an extensive social support network and prior contact with the mental health profession, was failed in a moment that she most needed help. On October 25, 1994, Susan Smith did not know how to deal with the emotional pain of her past or her immediate present. Why Susan Smith committed her crimes was only partially answered at her trial. Susan Smith had many more resources available to her than most young, single mothers, yet she chose to make a decision that remains incomprehensible.

Susan Smith had no prior history of violence or abuse toward her children or any signs of psychosis or biological disorder. Susan's act was a culmination of a disturbed and emotionally disordered life that resulted in the tragic murder of two innocent children.

PART THREE

Diane Downs:

Her Children Got in the Way of Her Love

Blood Splattered Auto

Even though the sun had long set over the verdant hills of
Springfield, Oregon, Thursday, May 19, 1983, remained as
warm at night as it had at noon. There was a quiet to the
evening, the kind of languishing stillness that sometimes
thresholds a storm. But, the night staff at McKenzie-
Willamette Hospital felt no oncoming torrent, and, after so-
many years fighting unpredictable emergencies they often
found themselves with an innate power to feel something
sinister in the air. And, the professionals they were, they
were always ready.

Nothing had pre-armed them, however, for the drama that
unfolded at their literal doorstep at approximately 10:48
p.m.

No warning had come until the red late-model Nissan
bearing Arizona license plates careened into the emergency
drop-off, bleating its horn to scare the devils from hell. The
skeleton night shift all heard it; their faces told them
immediately that what they had anticipated a quiet night in
ER was not to be. Dr. John Mackey, physician in charge,
and the two nurses Rose Martin and Shelby Day felt the
familiar adrenaline. Receptionist Judy Patterson rolled back
her typewriter ledge and quickly forgot about the routine
insurance forms she had been updating.

In the driveway, just beyond the double automatic doors of
ER, a blonde woman in her twenties waved them on; she
looked ashen in the fluorescent tube lighting, and she
wildly pointed to the interior of her car.

"Somebody just shot my kids!" was all she seemed to know
how to say. Patterson, hearing the mother's words, did what

she always did in emergencies involving violent crime: She dialed for the police.

Nurses Martin and Day teetered when they looked through the windows of the Nissan. Side panels were soaked in blood and amidst the blood lay three small children, one in the front passenger seat, two in the back. First glance told the nurses the children had been shot at very close range. A golden-haired child up front, a girl, couldn't have been any more than seven or eight, the RNs apprised; of the two in the rear, one was a girl, maybe a trifle older than the other, and a boy, merely a toddler.

This call was unexpected, and it was bad, very bad. Personnel from intensive care were summoned to assist ER, and a swat-like team of white-coat professionals including top surgeon Fred Wilhite volleyed to the scene as the trio of injured youngsters were carried in by weeping nurses and pale interns. As reinforcement came, Dr. Mackey explained the situation to them in two taut words, "Chest wounds!"

Two of the children still breathed, although strenuously; the boy gasped for air. The child found slumped in the front seat appeared beyond help; despite frantic efforts by the doctors at the operating table, the damage had been lethal. She was pronounced dead moments after being wheeled to Emergency.

Only later did the medics learn the children's names and ages Christie Downs, 8; Cheryl Ann Downs, 7; and Danny Downs, 3 but names and ages didn't matter yet; in fact, they were the least important factor of this hour, this night, this calamity. What mattered is that someone without a heart had deliberately attempted to murder three kids in cold blood, and, despite the odds, despite a fate that looked gloomy, the caretakers hastened to keep that fate at bay and beat it at its own game: with deliberate intention.

Skilled hands attended to the two operable victims. Feeling the children succumbing to severe blood loss and lack of oxygen, they performed tracheotomies on them to free the flowing blood and salvage much-needed air. Machines began to pump the little hearts and revitalized the other organs. Despite the children's fragile condition, Mackey and his experts kept them alive.

Diane Downs reenacting the crime for police investigators

Diane Downs giggles as she demonstrates her version of
how she got shot.

The Bushy-Haired Stranger (BHS) or just (BS)

Their mother, Diane, didn't supply an answer. She told hospital receptionist Patterson that she and her family had been driving home from visiting a friend in nearby Marcola when a man, a "bushy-haired stranger" type had waved down their car on a lonely span of highway. Thinking he needed help, Diane paused to inquire. And that was when, said a tearful Diane, the man pointed his gun through her car window and loosened its barrel on her three helpless offspring.

Both Springfield and Lane County police responded. To them she exacted the tale of the ambush and an odd description of the vagabond. Reacting to the story, the departments issued an emergency watch on the city and county roads, fearing that there might be a madman roaming the outskirts of Springfield, its lanes and byways. Squads drew into action and the area described by Diane as the point of attack in the vicinity of Marcola and Old Mohawk Road, a desolate spot became the center of a manhunt.

Since the crime was been purported to have occurred in the county, members of the Sheriff's Office for Lane County became principal investigators. Sergeant Robin Rutherford was the county's first man to approach the children's mother at the hospital. When he arrived, the nurses were tending to her arm, which bore a series of small, superficial wounds marked between the elbow and the wrist from where she had tried to ward off the gunman's blows. Seeing that Mrs. Downs' injuries were minor and that she seemed to be in an unusual state of calmness in fact, she seemed in full control of her senses he asked that she come with him to point out the exact spot, the best she could in the dark, of the crime.

The site she located by memory, near where two rural roads converged was, according to Ann Rule, a "most desolated spot (where) the river pushed by in the dark on one side; on the other, a field of wild phlox trembled in the wind..." It was not a spot a young woman with three children should have stopped her car to speak to a stranger.

When Diane returned to the hospital, she was given the terrible news about her middle child, Cheryl, as well as the status of her other two children. She took the news with grace, but her attitude stunned the hospital personnel who had expected her to turn hysterical; she seemed too accepting. When told that Danny had a chance of surviving, she replied in an almost-perplexed manner, "Do you mean the bullet missed his heart? Gee whiz!"

Diane Downs' BHS, as sketched by police artist.

The Investigation Begins

Detectives who spoke with her in a private room at McKenzie-Willamette were equally surprised at her attitude. One investigator, a sharp, keen-witted veteran of the county's homicide squad who was aptly named Dick Tracy, found her unlike other women whom he had encountered after similar crises. In fact, he later defined her as "very rational, considering what she had undergone." Together with his partner on the case, detective Doug Welch, who also found Diane Downs too stoic for a mother whose entire brood was just shot, Tracy conducted an interview to garner some personal background on the mother and her children as well as to begin building a chronology of events leading up to the shooting.

To that point, they had determined that the bullet's that had been fired at the kids were .22 caliber, shot from either a handgun or rifle; detectives suspected a handgun. Powder burns on the children's skin indicated that the weapon had been fired at an extremely close proximity, especially those on the deceased girl, Cheryl, who had been in the front seat. Blood splayed across the car's doors, seats, windows and elsewhere indicated that the murderer had discharged the gun from the left, or driver's side, which agreed with Diane's story claiming that the intruder had reached in through her window.

About the mother herself, the detectives learned that she was 27 years old, was a mail woman for the U.S. Postal Service and worked the Cottage Grove division. Having previously been a letter carrier in Chandler, Arizona, she recently divorced there (from a man named Steve Downs) and, after obtaining a work transfer, relocated to Oregon to be near her parents, Willa and Wes Frederickson. The

Fredericksons were former Arizonians who had moved to Oregon years earlier. Wes Frederickson was also a post office employee.

Diane sketched for her interviewers a quick history of that evening: According to Diane, she and her children had eaten a fast dinner at home, and then left their small duplex home at 1352 Q Street in Springfield, bound for a co-worker's home on rustic Sunderman Road. The friend, Heather Plourd, had told Diane a few days earlier at the workplace that she was thinking about buying a horse, and Diane had found an ad in the newspaper about horse rentals that she figured Heather might appreciate seeing. Not knowing Heather's phone number they weren't intimate friends Diane decided to bring the advertisement herself. The drive, she explained, offered a good opportunity to get the kids out of the stale house for a couple of hours.

On the way home after a brief chat with Heather and her husband, Diane thought that she would cut through Old Mohawk Road to the main highway. She thought it might be fun to go sightseeing; the kids enjoyed watching the moon from the unlit countryside. It was then, after she turned onto Old Mohawk, that she spotted the man. He was standing in the center of the gravel road, signaling, as if for help. She described the man as "white...in his late twenties...about five feet, nine, and 150 to 170...dark hair, a shag-wavy cut and stubble of a beard." He wore "a Levi jacket (and) an off-colored T-shirt."

She braked and got out of her car. It was then that the stranger produced a pistol from under his jacket and demanded that she turn over the keys to her automobile.

She refused, but in retaliation, said Diane, he reached past her in through the driver's window and opened fire on her family. When he then tried to reach for the car keys, she fought back, outstepping him. But, as she slipped back into her car, he fired one more time, at her now, striking her arm. Slamming the gas pedal, her Nissan sped off and away. Her children were hurt, she could see that, and thought only one thing: to get them to the hospital as quickly as possible.

Cheryl Downs

Suspicions

Tracy's mind had wandered a moment while Diane spoke. He had read the doctor's report on his treatment of Diane's arm injury: "A single bullet entered her left forearm...it split in two as it shattered the radius, and then exited, leaving two smaller wounds." As she related her getaway from the man on the road, how the bullet struck her arm, he couldn't help thinking that the place where she was wounded is the exact same place other killers have shot themselves to make it appear that they were attacked by a phony assailant.

But, he was not, would not! Pass judgment until the evidence was in. And that would not be for some time.

Before the interview ended, Diane agreed to sign a search warrant on her home. She admitted she owned a .38 caliber pistol, which she kept for protection on her delivery route, and a .22 caliber rifle for home safety, but both were unused. One lay cold, hidden under rags in her trunk, the other collected dust on a shelf in her home.

Meanwhile, police around the hospital were busy. In the driveway, they prepared the red Nissan Pulsar with the Arizona license plates for transporting to the crime lab for further investigation. In the morgue, Sergeant Jon Peckels photographed the wounds on the dead girl. Behind ER, detective Ray Poole collected evidentiary bloody clothing removed from all three children. All personnel assigned to this particular homicide knew, without a doubt, the weekend ahead would mean little leisure time and a lot of pounding on doors, question-asking and rattling of brain cells to figure out this confounding, irritating and heartbreaking mystery.

Because three helpless children had their bodies savagely blown open by a gunner, the policemen didn't mind the overtime one bit. They wanted the killer now.

*****

Several nurses and an investigator were bedside when Diane Downs was finally allowed into the intensive care unit to see Christie, one of her two surviving children. The spectators noted that, as she squeezed her daughter's hand, murmuring, "I love you," she did so as devoid of warmth as an icicle; her words were passed through clenched teeth. Paul Alton, the investigator, noticed something else: that the child's eyes, peeking from above an oxygen mask, took on the glaze of fear when spotting her mom approaching.

"I happened to glance at the heart rate monitor the pulse when Diane came in," said he. "The scope showed Christie's heart was beating 104 times a minute (but) when Diane took hold of her...that scope jumped to 147!"

*****

Friday morning, plainclothesmen checked with the Plourds to ensure Diane and her kids had visited them the previous evening as Diane had asserted. Mrs. Plourd confirmed the visitation, as well as the reason for it: to give her an ad about horses.

Under the supervision of Tracy and Kurt Welch, state troopers searched Diane's Springfield residence, requisitioning several items, including a diary that they found, the aforementioned rifle (a Glenfield .22 caliber located where Diane had said) and a box of standard .22 caliber shells, same as those taken from the children's bodies.

Diane Downs

One particular item, however, interested Dick Tracy: a photo of a young man in a beard that shared space atop the television with other pictures of Diane. Tracy was cognizant of the fact that Diane had made a phone call to a man in Arizona, a former boyfriend supposedly, not long after arriving at the hospital. Before she knew the state of her children, before alerting her ex-husband and the father of the children, she acted as if compelled to call this Arizona man.

Tracy, studying the photo of the man, wondered if he was looking at the object of Diane's urgent phone call.

Interesting Side Bars

Fred Hugi of the District Attorney's staff sensed something foul almost immediately after being assigned by County DA Pat Horton to prosecute the case. In preparation for what the DA knew would eventually lead to a murder trial, it was Hugi's job to follow the revelations of the case as they surfaced from the origin. As far as Hugi quickly ascertained, the fetus of something evil had taken form in the embryonic blackness of that rural roadway in Lane County. Whatever happened Thursday night, the facts began to come to light in a most suspicious manner and unlike those explained by the mother, Diane Downs.

Hugi, relatively new to the DA's investigative squad, nevertheless knew mischief when he saw it. And he saw it first in the faces of two perplexed, scared youngsters, strapped to tubes and cords for life in a lowly lit hospital room. Never one for sentiment, even he was surprised when he felt tears rolling down his cheeks as he gazed upon Christie and Danny Downs. And when he heard from Paul Alton the reaction of Christie when she had seen her mother for the first time since the shooting, he knew it was not the normal reaction of any child who, in pain and surrounded by foreign faces, would have been overjoyed to see the one person in their life to rekindle their spirits.

Hugi ordered a round-the-clock guard on the children. He also commissioned a child psychologist to remain at Christie's side during the day, to build up a trust that the child may, when more hale, confide in her the events on Mohawk Road.

Doubt in the mother's story was building. Over the coming days, her version of what happened that night changed slightly. Her placement of the killer when he fired the gun altered in several re-tellings as did her own actions in the face of the supposed gunman. When Doug Welch interviewed Steve Downs, Diane's ex-husband in Arizona, Welch learned that Diane owned three, not two, weapons and one was a .22 caliber handgun, which Diane did not mention.

Welch found Steve Downs an open, erstwhile talker who seemed glad to be rid of his ex wife whom, he said, liked to bed-hop. An electrical contractor living in Chandler, Arizona, he carried no grudge and seemed to be happy just to live his current bachelor life. He admitted that he and Diane were "still friends," but that their occasional phone conversations never extended beyond the kid's health and scholastic welfare. He seemed genuinely upset with the bad news and sincerely, fatherly hopeful that Christie and Danny would pull through. He made immediate plans to fly to Oregon to see them.

Welch asked Steve Downs if he knew who the Arizona man might be, and the former spouse, not surprised by the question, replied that he must mean the married guy with whom Diane had been having a torrid affair for some time before leaving Arizona. He was a postal worker in Chandler and, whatever happened in their love life, the tryst finally severed. The man returned to his understanding wife, but Diane still seemed to carry the torch, hot and heavy. Her infatuation with this married man was maniacal, it seemed, but he didn't seem the type to leave a doting wife for a woman with three growing, hungry kids.

When Welch asked about weapons the couple had owned, and which ones Diane had taken with her to Oregon, Downs told him that Diane had "a .22 rifle, a .38 revolver and a .22 Ruger Mark IV nine-shot semi-automatic pistol."

She used to practice her shooting at the local Chandler-area range. Why she carried guns? She was a woman and felt she needed protection on her route, Steve Downs suggested.

Then detective Welch felt he had to ask the obvious: "Steve, would your ex-wife harm your kids in order to get [the married] back?"

"No way!" the other shook his head. "She loves those kids."

When questioned afterwards, Diane denied she still owned the .22 caliber.

Evidence Begins to Tell the Tale

No one in the DA's office, especially Fred Hugi, believed that there had been an aggressor on Old Mohawk Road. Since the beginning of time, wrongdoers have used mythical abductors and thugs as alibis to cover their own or a close friend's crime. In law enforcement jargon, these make-believe violators are niched under the all-encompassing term bushy-haired stranger, "the guy who isn't there," says author Ann Rule, "the man the defendant claims is really responsible...Of course the BHS can never be produced in court."

Rule points to a satirical remark authored by Hugi in the midst of the Downs case. Hugi had side mouthed, "We estimate that if the BHS is ever caught, the prison doors will have to be opened to let out all the wrongly convicted defendants."

Paul Alton, Hugi's central fact-finder, summed up his and the investigator's misgivings: "I don't buy it...She goes out to Sunderman to see Heather Plourd, she decides to go sightseeing and heads toward Marcola...Suddenly, she decides she'll veer off on the Old Mohawk Road. Say we buy the story that she's sightseeing. Even if it's almost pitch dark, she's sightseeing...How do we explain that the shooter knew she was going to be there? If he's following her in his own car...he could trail her onto Old Mohawk. But she tells us that the stranger is [in front of her, standing in the road] waving her down. How does he get there?"

To the trained hawkshaw's eyes, the picture was incorrect incomplete even retouched. If the killer wanted the car, wouldn't he have shot the driver (Diane) first? She was the adult and would have been his biggest obstacle, not the three tiny kids huddling in the car. What would a "bushy-haired stranger" have to gain in shooting Christie, Cheryl and Danny Downs?

Over the weekend, forensic scientist James O. Pex from the Oregon State Police Department had examined the interior of the Downs automobile to produce some thoughtful findings. As reported to Hugi and his squad, Pex had found a couple of .22 caliber U-shell copper casings, ejected after firing. No bullet had penetrated the body of the car, indicating that all bullets between the children they suffered five bullet wounds had hit their live marks. Blood smeared the side door of the front seat where Cheryl had tumbled after being shot, and pools of blood stained the rear seat where Danny and Christie had been hit. But, Pex said, "No blood at all on the driver's side, no smears on the steering wheel."

If a bullet had hit Diane as she was getting into her car, as she said, it would have been reflex for her to grab that wound with her idle hand. There would have been blood on that hand, then, as she tried to steer the car from the scene, blood on the steering wheel.

Also: When a bullet is fired, he explained, the barrel discharges a small amount of smokeless gunpowder foreword towards the target. Such powder particles were detected in three angles of the car on the right panel and in a sweep along the back seat. There were no particles, however, on the driver's panel.

What did all this mean? It could very well mean that whoever did the shooting had been seated in the driver's seat.

And that Diane Downs shot herself just before she reached the hospital.

Diane's Letters

A scouring of the entire crime area had failed to produce
the murder weapon, but ejected casings from a spent .22
caliber (matching those in the car) were discovered in the
vicinity. Divers even plunged into the Mohawk River,
which runs through the topography, but could not find the
gun. Unfortunately, the river churned here and ran a rapid
course that time of year, in the spring, and experts
determined that had the gun been tossed into the waters, it
would have been flushed away miles on the river's current.
Hugi, who figured the courts hadn't much of a case against
Diane Downs without the murder weapon, even went to
look for the gun himself. He waded along the river, turned
over loose stones, kicked through the reed grass, and
scuffed the toe of his shoe through the ditch alongside the
road to upturn loose soil but nothing.

To sink his spirits further, he learned that Christie Downs
had suffered a stroke, a direct symptom of the gunshot
wound. Her speech was distorted and, the physicians told
him, she may never speak again. The left side of the brain,
the side that controlled the ability to speak, had been
injured. But, there was hope, albeit slight. Doctors prayed
that, because she was so young, they could reverse the
deterioration with therapy and restore her slurring tongue.

There was no gun to condemn Diane. And perhaps the only
live witness to the murder, the murderer's own daughter,
would be unable to accuse her mother. But Hugi more than
ever believed that Diane was guilty when he was shown the
diary and the letters confiscated from her home. They both
reeked of a longing for the Arizona man, her lost love, a
man who, by the tone of the pages, had deserted her. The
cause of his desertion may have been and the diary hinted

this that his wife had simply stepped in to put the clamps down.

One passage caught Hugi's attention. It was dated April 21, less than a month before the crime on Mohawk Road. Like so many entries, it was written in the form of a letter addressed to someone else, but used as a meter to weigh her own thoughts on such a thing. This passage, like most of the others, was addressed to her former lover, and read:

"What happened? I'm so confused. What could she have said or done to make you act this way? I spoke to you this morning for the last time. It broke my heart to hear you say 'don't call or write'. ...I still think of you as my best friend and my only lover, and you keep telling me to go away and find somebody else. You have got to be kidding..."

Hugi resolved to get to the bottom of this business. He kept asking himself, who is he, and is he involved in any way in the murder scheme? He doubted it, but yet he could not get over the feeling that her obsession with this ex-boyfriend had driven her to lift that gun against her own children. They were obstacles in the path of singly obtaining him and if he was correct in his guesswork, would the man's wife be Diane's next victim?

Diane's letters were visions of fantasies; they spoke of masturbation engendered by thoughts of her one true lover.

In one letter, between references to sexual self-pleasure, she rhymes:

"I love you more/than could your wife/yet it's brought sorrow/to my life/I just keep hoping/and hanging on/How much longer/can I be strong?"

Perhaps she could "be strong" no longer, Hugi wondered.

Before the weekend ended, he dispatched two of his investigators to Chandler, Arizona, to find out who this man of her wet dreams really was.

Danny Downs

The week of May 23rd was a sad one, yet it brought optimism. Cheryl Downs' funeral took place on the 25th to much bereavement from family, intimate friends and the Springfield community. But, yet good news came from McKenzie-Willamette Hospital: both Christie and Danny were out of danger. One of Christie's arms was paralyzed and her speech was garbled for now, albeit doctors believed capable of being revitalized; Danny would probably be crippled for the rest of his life, but his brain had not been affected and he would live.

Both kids had been lucky, totally-against-the-odds lucky.

Diane in Wonderland

Doug Welch and Paul Alton were dispatched to Arizona to use their professional experience to dig up Diane Downs' past and anyone, including Lew Lewiston, who came along with the shovel work. Their trip during the last weeks of May proved fruitful. They learned just what they wanted to know about their central suspect, Ms. Diane Downs.

One of the first things they accomplished was proving that neither Steve Downs nor the mysterious Lew were Diane's "bushy-haired stranger". Witnesses verified seeing them or being in their company in Arizona at the precise hour of the crime.

The detectives also spoke with several of Diane's former co-workers from the Chandler branch post office. Their opinions of her varied. Some, it was clear, didn't like her at all; no one praised her. "Some of the informants describe a woman with a single-mindedness, a channeling of ambition that they had rarely, if ever, encountered," pens Ann Rule in Small Sacrifices. "Others disagreed; Diane Downs had been flippy dippy, up and down, mad and sad. A few a very few witnesses spoke on her behalf, and then only with faint praise."

What emerged after the postal interviews was a postcard picture that might have been beautiful had its colors not run together. She appeared to be a headstrong woman, but headstrong in a tilted way; her priorities were overblown and, most of all, out of sync. She jumped in the sack with men right and left, but refused to deliver copies of Playboy to customers on her route.

Lew Lewiston worked at the Chandler station, too, but the investigators interviewed him separately, at his home. To his credit, they liked him; they liked his honesty and directness. He insisted that his wife, Nora, be there at his side while he candidly discussed even his sexual experiences with his old flame. Nora, he said, knew the history and had forgiven him. The couple had reconciled and Lew Lewiston wanted nothing more to do with Diane Downs.

While the memory of his extramarital affair was undoubtedly painful to him, he answered the detective's questions cordially and succinctly. He had met Diane at work in late 1981 after her divorce from Steve Downs. Lew was magnetized by the female's sexy gestures and her revealing clothing. Loving his wife Nora, Lew was nonetheless taken with this new girl at the mail bin who blared easy virtue in loose midriff and sans bra. Their friendship evolved overnight into a string of sleazy hotel room encounters.

Lew admittedly expected the affair to end swiftly as had all her relationships none of them had lasted with other men he knew she had gone with. But as the months rolled on, he found that she was not intending to let go; in fact, she was pulling tight on his private time and urging him to divorce Nora as soon as possible. Suddenly, it dawned on him he was up and over in a relationship he never intended to move from off the bedsprings.

He tried to break their seeing each other, but each time Diane protested violently.

"The affair continued and continued," Lew said, "and I was with Diane all day at work, and I'd be with her all night long and it was every day for months. I basically didn't have time to think, you know. I was with Diane all the time."

Welch and Alton then noted something that Lewiston added that hit a high-note because it complemented what their boss Fred Hugi had been contemplating all along that the Downs children may have gotten in the way of their mother's love life. Despite her pleas, he refused to see her when she was with Danny, Christie and Cheryl. "I wouldn't be with her if the children were around," he explained. "It was an affair it didn't seem right."

After battling guilt for many months, Lew decided to say adios to Diane. The girlfriend's remonstrations had been incessant, and one night in February, 1983, Lew severed them. "Diane asked me who I loved the most her or Nora. I said I loved Nora. She blew up. She ranted and raved and screamed at me. I'd never seen anyone act that way before."

When Lew raced home, Diane followed him, even up the steps of his own home with Nora present.

"She pounded on our door all night long," Lew's wife recalled. "Then she called on the phone." But, she reappeared the following day, confronting Nora on the stoop. "She began to tell me what I should do about my marriage, my relationship with Lew everything...I slammed the door in her face."

It had been what Lew called "the final straw" and he never saw her again.

Not long after that chaotic night, Diane put in a transfer to Oregon. She relocated to Springfield to be near her parents.

But, the letters and the phone calls to Lew continued.

One thing more, the lawmen asked Lew if he had any knowledge about guns that Diane might have owned. He did. One of them, he said, was a .22 caliber handgun.

But, Diane continued to deny she owned it.

Elizabeth Diane Downs

Diane Downs was born August 7, 1955, in Phoenix,
Arizona. Her parents Willadene and Wes Frederickson
named her Elizabeth Diane. (As the years passed she
trimmed her name to simply Diane.) Having wed as teens
and still in their teens when Diane came along, the parents
awed at their having a human life to maintain; and while
they loved their baby, they fell short in their ability to
emanate a warm fondness a child inherently expects.

As a school student, Diane was bright but not one of the in-
crowd. Disciplining, old-time-Baptist parents forbade
trendy clothing and fads, resulting in their daughter being
considered a washout. Wherever she went, she was the
"square," the ugly duckling.

According to Rule's Small Sacrifices, Diane's father
allegedly molested her when she was 11 years old. Diane
told authorities that the occurrences never led to
fornication, but she was fondled and caressed. On
weekends, Diane claimed that he took her on rides to the
desert; once away from civilization, he would make her
remove her blouse and bra as he watched.

Diane said that these perversions ended as quietly as they
had begun, and Wes Frederickson became more of a typical
father as if cessation would eradicate all memories. He
allowed her to enroll in a charm school when she was
fourteen. And that was the beginning of a new Diane, one
who with her hair cut stylishly and her garb up to date the
local boys began to notice. And Diane, hungry for love by
this time, responded by being the babe with the flashy eyes,
swaying hips and silly, come-hither giggle.

Steven Downs, one of the boys at Moon Valley High, fell instantly in love with the pretty and now suddenly shapely blonde, Diane. The pair became an item and roved together, everywhere they went, arm linked in arm. After graduation, they parted for a spell he to the Navy, she to Pacific Coast Baptist Bible College. They corresponded regularly, but if Diane had promised to "save it" for Steve, she had weakened, for she was expelled from the religious school after a year for promiscuity.

Steve returned home and the couple wed on November 13, 1973.

From the starting gun, the marriage was, at best, shaky. Steve worked half the time and Diane found her high school sweetheart less a noble escape and more of a repetition of her domineering papa. She had wanted love and realized too late that Steve was not that love.

She found solace when she became pregnant; carrying a baby made her feel for the first time that she was actually in charge of a love that was all-dependent on her. It was a feeling of power she'd never before realized, and she relished in the delight that she was the helmswoman of her own path to total love. But, after Christie was born in October, 1974, it was back to serving Steve his meals never mind that she had a baby to care for and worked part-time at a local thrift store, too. To keep from falling apart emotionally, she needed to feel that emotion once again of the seed of love stirring inside her. She again became pregnant. Cheryl Lynn followed her older sister into this world on January, 1976.

Unhappily Married

Throughout 1976 and 1977, Diane took the kids and ran away from Steve several times, but she always came back. Steve would hunt her down to one of her many relative's homes. But, once reunited, it was monkey-chasing-weasel time all over again. He was unhappy, she was unhappy, but the marriage waned on.

"(Diane) waited for something to happen," writes Rule. "Hostile but passive, she was both bored and angry. Life was passing quickly by her; none of the things she promised herself had come true."

She decided again to conceive but not Steve's baby. By that time, 1978, the family had moved to Mesa where both Diane and Steve worked for the same mobile home manufacturer. On the assembly line Diane found her "stud," whom she passionately seduced. Her tummy swelled again and she floated in wonderland, drugged on love. Danny was born four days after Christmas, 1979.

Even though the child was not his, Steve accepted the boy as his own. Still, the marriage had reached its ebb and, within a year, the Downses decided to divorce. Diane moved in with the father of Danny, and it was during this time she began to change. Now out of the wifely manacles imposed by society and the Baptists, she seemed to ignore her duties as mother, also. The opiate of her children's love had worn off. She preferred to work, to stay away from home, to throw the youngsters on any babysitter she could find.

One sitter relates an incident that, even though she didn't know it at the time, foreshadowed tragedy. "Diane put everything before those kids. If Danny wanted attention, she would push him away...but the worst thing was one time, I caught Cheryl jumping on the bed, and I said that was not permitted. I made her sit in a chair and think about it. Cheryl sat quietly for a while, and then she looked up. 'Do you have a gun here?' 'Of course not. Why?' 'I want to shoot myself. My mom says I'm bad.'"

Diane finally found a full-time position with the U.S. Post Office in 1981 and was stationed in Chandler. It was there she met Lew Lewiston and fell in love. But, for once, it was the other party, not Diane, to make the decision when and where the love affair would end.

As she had done mentally to her own kids, Lew physically walked out of her life.

Caught unawares, she ran home to Oregon, but not quite understanding, nor acceptant of the fact, that this time she didn't have it her way.

Loose Threads

In June, Assistant DA Fred Hugi met with his investigative squad to review its findings. Whether or not to arrest Diane Downs was the issue unsettled. He wanted to see her taken in, but not at the expense of the county office, which would take extreme heat were the case thrown out in pre-trial. Nevertheless, Hugi and his men were convinced she was guilty, but they feared that without the presence of a murder weapon or a viable witness who literally saw her do the shooting, much of what they had gathered to date would be, in all fairness, considered circumstantial evidence and unacceptable in an American courtroom.

Not enough to convict.

The team examined what they had collected so far, among the evidence a small number of .22 caliber bullet casings found on Old Mohawk Road, a very graphic display of carnage in Diane's red Nissan Pulsar, the estimation of the bullet's paths from an accepted authority, a diary that screamed Diane's obsession for ex-lover, her letters colored with pornographic daydreams, and testimony from two men (Steve Downs and former lover) who swore she indeed owned something she continued to disclaim: a .22 caliber handgun.

The most expressive piece of evidence came from the pen of forensic expert Jim Pex who wrote that it was his estimation that some of the unfired 22 caliber shells found in Diane's home had once been worked through the mechanism of the same gun that shot the children. Impressive this, but until the very gun was retrieved, Hugi knew, the court could refute it.

Investigators had also been able to shed doubt on Diane's story that she immediately raced for the hospital after the attack on her kids. By testimony of hospital personnel, she arrived outside ER that fateful night at roughly 10:48 p.m., screaming. "Somebody just shot my kids!" Estimated time she had left the Plourds' home was, according to Heather Plourd herself, 9:45 p.m. The detectives knew that the shooting, then, must have occurred at approximately 10:15 in order to give Diane enough time to re-gather her senses, survey the condition of her kids, then drive (as she had claimed) immediately to McKenzie-Willamette Hospital to reach it by 10:48 p.m. But, in the meantime, a witness had come forward; explaining that he had seen what he was sure was Diane's red Nissan, near 10:20 p.m., moving very slowly five to seven miles an hour along Old Mohawk Road.

"The car," said witness Joseph Inman, "wasn't being driven critically."

Another telling tale, but, so far...just a tale.

But, the legal wheels behind Hugi believed also that Diane was guilty, and the DA maneuvered the wheels to spin to show his support of the long hours his assistant was dedicating to catch a child killer. In Lane County, a grand jury assembled behind closed doors. The panelists wanted to hear directly from those main players that list of testifiers that Hugi had given the DA among them her former lover, Mr. Inman, Heather Plourd, Jim Pex and others, eventually Diane Downs herself.

Other positive things were happening. County Judge Gregory Foote placed the two surviving Downs youngsters in the protective custody of the state's child services bureau. This meant that, for the meantime, Diane was not allowed to see her kids. That she felt she was being treated like a criminal was, in reality, a nose-thumb by Hugi after she violently threatened to remove the children from the hospital and take them away if detectives wouldn't stop hounding her.

Danny, still confined to his bed, was given full protection by the police department until he would be medically released, at which time he would follow his sibling into a suitable foster family. The home where Christie was transported was kept a secret, her whereabouts known by only a few authorities.

"Princess Die"

In the middle of the grand jury's summons process and the ongoing search for more evidence, in particularly the vanished gun, the sheriff's office announced layoffs. State funds dropped and Paul Alton was laid off. Doug Welch and another of Hugi's top men, Kurt West, were given a month's notice. All of Hugi's investigators, in fact, were let go or redeployed.

Throughout the coming winter and into the spring of 1984, Diane was fast becoming the media's favorite star. Newshounds had picked up on her plight. Some medium distrusted her, but to most she was a bouncy maiden maybe not in distress but picked on by mean old Uncle Sam who couldn't find the bushy-haired beast of mythology. Because she looked a little like Princess Diana, she became the darling fashion plate of the American Pacific Coast.

Less trivial papers called her "Princess Die."

But, Hugi saw her as anything but a princess, a good or a bad one. She was more like the wicked witch, creating havoc at every point in life. Her kids had been swept from her custody, she was indignant, and sought revenge. She balked to the press that she was misunderstood, was a victim of prejudice and harassment. Ignoring her bravado, Hugi let her talk, refusing to back down. For that matter, he endeavored to bite her every footstep. And that is why he chose to let investigators Welch and West turn up the heat before they surrendered to the layoff. They dogged her.

Finally, Diane Downs called for what she hoped would turn into a peace treaty, a meeting with the two detectives to explain her side of the story and pass on further information she had not divulged since the night of the attack on Old Mohawk Road. At first, the detectives bought it, hoping this new revelation might produce something startlingly new. But, sensing they were being conned, the session led to what would become known, according to Ann Rule, as "the hardball interview."

At the parley, Diane explained that she believed the killer was someone she might have known; he had called her by name. If true, this information would have made a great impact on the entire case. But, to the two men gathered in their office with her, it was a clear charade, an attempt to delay the proceedings she felt moving against her and possibly even throw the investigators off her trail altogether. Insulted, her listeners turned the table and fell upon Diane verbally with such an interrogation that she was left the deceived instead of the deceiver.

Why was she telling them this now? She didn't know. How did he know what road she was going to take home from Heather's? She didn't know. Was he a friend from Oregon or Arizona? She didn't know. What purpose would he have to kill her kids? She didn't know. Did she really rush to the hospital immediately after the kids were shot or did she pause a while? She didn't know. Why didn't she try to stop the gunman when he began blasting away at the kids in the Nissan? She didn't know the answer to that either.

And when they asked her point blank if she tried to kill her kids because they ruined her chances with her lover...well, she had an answer to that. She called them names and threatened them and told them they were all "fed up". And stormed out.

Whether or not it was a ploy for sympathy just in case she needed some in the event of a jury trial or whether she merely needed to feel that "love" once again within her she went out and got pregnant, once again from one of her favorite studs. She made sure to explain the symbolic meaning of her action to a TV reporter: "I got pregnant because I miss Christie, and I miss Danny and I miss Cheryl so much...You can't replace children but you can replace the effect that they give you. And they give me love, they give me satisfaction, they give me stability, they give me a reason to live and a reason to be happy..."

And a reason to perhaps escape death row, Hugi sneered, watching her performance on the tube.

Paula Krogdahl, the counselor put in charge of mentally raising Christie from her nightmares was making excellent progress in the meantime. The child began to talk, to remember, to face reality. While Krogdahl tiptoed through her treatment, avoiding the murder scenario for a long time, she got Christie to speak about her family life, and her mother. Christie admitted that Diane had hit her and her brother and sister "lots". And when the day had come, the therapist asked her to recall what happened the night of what Christie called "that terrible thing":

"Was there anyone there that night that you didn't know?" asked Krogdahl, referring to the stranger on the dark road.

"No," the girl answered.

"Were Danny and Cheryl crying?"

"No."

"Why wasn't Cheryl crying?"

"...dead."

A pause, then, softly:

"Do you know who was shooting, Christie?"

"I think" But Christie could not muster the words. Krogdahl didn't push and let it go, for now.

Hugi decided to bite the bullet. Experts told him that he had enough evidence, and they believed he had a strong case. But, he would need to have to recreate that "terrible thing" in court, piece all the puzzle fragments together in such a way so that the panel of jurors saw what he saw and totally believe.

The grand jury was wrapping up after nine months of interviews; they had spoken to, quizzed, and deliberated on the words of many including Diane Downs and balanced at the end of those nine months the tomes of testimony they possessed. They handed down an indictment: one charge of murder, two charges of attempted murder, and two charges of criminal assault.

The state of Oregon was going for the child killer's throat.

Diane Downs, escorted by police

On February 28, 1984, police cuffed Diane as she was
alighting from her car in the parking lot of the post office.

Preparing for Battle

District Attorney Pat Horton, along with Lane County Sheriff David Burks, hosted a press conference following Diane's arrest. Horton told the press, "The one thing that underscored this investigation is patience. The real battle...is in the courtroom."

Reporters were there by the droves, salivating over the battle indeed to come. Their newspapers and their magazines already announced that Diane Downs had been taken into custody and that, hell, the look-alike Princess Di might very well be a murderess after all. Time magazine was there, and the Washington Post was there, and journalists from city papers as far away as New York City were there. Most were professional in their reporting, while some, tabloid-like, tumbled across both Springfield, Oregon, and Chandler, Arizona, finding anyone who knew Diane Downs, or even talked to her once.

When the Eugene Register-Guard found Diane's father, Wes Frederickson, the paper noted he was gallant to the end: "If my daughter did it, then I believe, in fact, she should pay. But nothing can take away the love a father has for his kids."

In the wake of the impending trial, Diane sought as her counselor the brilliant and highly esteemed attorney Melvin Belli; because of the high profile the Downs case generated, Belli wanted to take it on. But he had personal plans, unbreakable, and would defend Diane only if the trial could be postponed a couple of months after the already-slated May 1984 calendar. The courts refused to budge. Hugi had waited long enough and delaying it might mean delaying it again for the pregnant Diane to give birth.

Too much work had been expended, too many people's time to delay the inevitable.

"Fred Hugi had twenty-four volumes of evidence, statements, follow-ups, transcriptions of tapes a mountain of possibilities to be winnowed down, and shaped, and molded for his case," asserts Ann Rule in Small Sacrifices. "He would work eighteen- to twenty-four hour days. And so would the rest of his team."

Diane was forced to find another lawyer quickly. She chose criminal attorney Jim Jagger, a man noted for his down-home but effective manner.

What was to be a six-week trial opened May 10, 1984 in Eugene at the Lane County Courthouse, courtroom Number 3, the largest of the rooms of justice in the old building. The jury panel consisted of nine women. Judge Foote, the man who had taken Christie and Danny Downs from their suspect mother, presided. Young, intense, he was noted for his fairness.

The citizenry of the county turned out for the sensation; people across America were still divided over the guilt/innocence of Diane Downs was she a martyr or a devil? And those no-names who shared the spectator's seats with the paparazzi, the witnesses and the families felt honored.

In his opening remarks, Fred Hugi presented a motive her fixation for a married man who felt that her kids should not be part of their fantasy life and a method the .22 caliber Ruger pistol that she bought in Arizona and denied having owned in Oregon. He read passages from her diary screaming her love for a man who didn't want her as she wanted him; and, to some titillation of the court, he read aloud Diane's masturbation poem. He promised to paint over the next weeks a real picture of the cruelty that made Diane Downs tick.

Counsel for the defense Jagger conceded, in turn, that there had been an obsession, but not so dark as to have led his client to destroy the three people she loved most in the world even beyond lover her own children. He pointed to her childhood, to her alleged molestation as a child, even to her promiscuity that he saw as a relevance to that dysfunctional experience. But, a murderess? No, for he intended to show that Diane's story of a man on the Mohawk Road with a gun was not a falsehood.

Courtroom proceedings paused on May 14 so that the jurors could experience for themselves the physical scene of the crime. Hugi transported them via a chartered bus to Old Mohawk Road, parallel to the river. Though daylight, the prosecutor accentuated the state of the road at the time of the shootings, relating the ebony of that night, the loneliness, the sparks of gunfire that shattered the gloom, the high emotion. Before the day ended, jurors were then led to the county auto pound to see the red Nissan death car; he wanted them to gaze into its interior and to feel the kid's terror.

An older Diane Downs

Heartbroken Witness

Back in court during the week, the first of the state's witnesses were brought forth they comprised mostly personnel from McKenzie-Willamette Hospital where Cheryl Downs died and where doctors struggled to save the other two Downs children.

Nurse Rose Martin recalled mother Diane's peculiar attitude toward what had just happened. "She asked how the children were, and I told her the doctors were in there working on them," Martin remembered. "And then she the mother laughed, and she said, 'Only the best for my kids!' and she laughed again and said, 'Well, I have good insurance.'"

Dr. John Mackey, who was in charge of ER the evening of the murder, described the children's chest wounds and the medical team's first, spontaneous efforts of life saving. He then recollected his observation of Diane: "She was extremely composed. She was unbelievably composed. I couldn't believe she was a family member. There were no tears...no disbelief...no, 'Why did this happen to me?'"

X-ray Technician Carleen Elbridge could not get over the fact that Diane, a mother of three severely wounded youngsters, complained about having to be seen in public without makeup.

Throughout the trial, witnesses came and went, each making an impact, some more than others. But, the highpoint the turning point, the riveting point came when Christie Downs was brought to the stand. Quivering, tear-streaked she was ushered to the stand by Fred Hugi. It was clear that he detested the moment, to bring a child face on against her mother, but the moment was needed if American Justice was to be played out.

Hugi, pale, jaw tight, but with a fatherly voice, led the examination of little Christie Downs. From time to time, he handed her Kleenex while she paused to wipe her cheeks; he waited until she regained herself whenever she broke down; usually after her eyes and her mother's momentarily met; he didn't rush her, and he remained gentle. When she spoke, and her voice might be muffled under her sobs, he clarified the question so that the jurors would completely understand the tintinnabulation of that tiny voice.

He loved this little child; it was obvious in the way he looked at her, spoke to her.

The courtroom inhaled, and didn't seem to exhale until it was over. And then especially then breath came short.

Hugi began by explaining to the girl the importance of telling the truth on the stand; she understood. Giving her time to relax, and her voice to become sufficiently audible to the courtroom, he then asked her several routine questions about her family, her schooling, herself.

Feeling that she was ready for the heavy stuff, he maneuvered into the day of the crime, her visit with her family to Heather Plourd's home on Sunderman Road in order to give Mrs. Plourd the clipping from the newspaper about horse rentals.

Christie was visibly shaken. Hugi patted her shoulder and gave her a reassuring smile. He gave her a moment to recover before proceeding. Reassuring that she was OK, he resumed his line of questioning about what Diane did with her children.

"She leaned over to the back seat and shot Danny," Christie said.

"What happened then? Hugi prompted her. "What happened after Danny got shot?"

The child caved in under her tears, and Hugi hugged her. Knowing this must come and wanting to get it over with, he gave her time to find her voice once again. Then quietly, sympathetically he went on. He gingerly rephrased his question, for by this time the court had already gathered what Diane Downs did after she shot Danny.

"Do you remember when you got shot?" Hugi asked her.

"Yeah," she answered.

"Who shot you?"

"My mom," she said simply.

Guilty As Sin

After that pathetic moment, the tone for the rest of the trial was set. Everything else, all other words, were anticlimactic. Diane Downs was as guilty as sin. Outside the walls of the courtroom, too, Americans who had refused to believe that a mother could consciously pull a trigger on three harmless children, her children, surrendered. She had been vilified, justly, and the cross that they thought was being nailed together to crucify a martyr became suddenly an instrument of deserved justice.

On June 14, 1984, Judge Foote read aloud the jury's unanimous verdict. Guilty of attempted murder in the first degree. Guilty of a second account of attempted murder in the first degree. Guilty of first-degree assault. Guilty of another count of first-degree assault. Guilty of murder.

Oregon at the time did not impose the death sentence, but in the subsequent sentencing, the judge sought to deprive Diane Downs from the daylight of liberty forevermore. After decreeing a life term, plus an additional fifty years for using a firearm, he expressed, "The Court hopes the defendant will never again be free. I've come as close to that as possible."

*****

Between the verdict and the sentencing, the court recessed while Diane gave birth to a beautiful child, whom she named Amy. The father of the baby denied her and, in time, a caring family adopted Amy.

Diane Downs Wanted Poster

In 1987, Diane briefly escaped from the Oregon Women's Correctional Center, where she had been incarcerated. After her recapture, she was transported to the high-maximum Clinton Correctional Institution in New Jersey. Today she sits in the Valley Prison for Women in Chowchilla, California. She will be up for parole in 2006.

Diane's former lover and his wife remain happily married.

Steve Downs still lives in Oregon.

The children, Christie and Danny, survived the ordeal. Danny is confined to a wheelchair, but is a happy boy. Christie has grown into a very content teenager. Both consider the ending of their story to be happy-ever-after.

In 1986, they moved into the home of their new loving adopted parents, Fred and Joanne Hugi.

PART FOUR

Marybeth Tinning:

The True Definition of a MOMSTER

It is a crime that is unthinkable for most people because the thought of losing one's own child is a life-long subconscious fear for parents. That may help explain why there is little public sympathy for one who commits this type of crime. Though courts may be willing to listen to explanations from the accused, usually there is no forgiveness. Smith received a life sentence without parole while Yates was sentenced to life with a chance at parole in the year 2040. A cursory review of such cases shows a similar pattern of long prison sentences. One of the most extraordinary cases of child murder in 20th century America took place in Schenectady, N.Y. But unlike the Smith and Yates cases in which the victims were killed during one tragic incident, these events took place over a period of nearly fourteen years. On February 5, 1986, Marybeth Tinning, 43, a local housewife and former school bus operator, was arrested and charged with the murder of her 4-month-old daughter, Tami Lynne. As crime stories go, Mrs. Tinning's tale would have barely made the 6 o'clock news.

Marybeth Tinning

But Marybeth Tinning was a familiar sight in Schenectady's trauma centers. She usually came running into one of the city's emergency rooms, confused and hysterical, typically with one of her babies cradled in her arms, either dead or near dead. The medical staff knew Marybeth well. Some hated her. Others felt great sorrow and pity for her. That's because from January 3, 1972, the day her daughter Jennifer died, until December 20, 1985, when Tami Lynne was found dead in her home, all nine of Marybeth Tinning's children died suddenly and usually without any rational explanation.

And no one knew why.

The Early Years, Marriage and Children

Marybeth Roe was born on September 11, 1942, in Duanesburg, New York. Duanesburg is the westernmost town in Schenectady County, consisting of 73.5 square miles as a predominantly agrarian town bounded on the north by Montgomery County, on the west and southwest by Schoharie County and on the south by Albany County. Duanesburg is the picture perfect little town that they could make postcards of.

As a child Marybeth was just your average Duanesburg child. She had plenty of friends and was an average student at Duanesburgh High School. After graduation she worked at various jobs until she settled in as a nursing assistant at Ellis Hospital in Schenectady, New York.

In 1963, at the age of 21, Marybeth met Joe Tinning on a blind date. Joe worked for General Electric as did Marybeth's father. He had a quiet disposition and was easy going. The two dated for several months. The future looked promising for Marybeth, a good job a great man and plans for a beautiful future. In 1965 they married and started building that future.

Marybeth Tinning once said that there were two things she wanted from life- to be married to someone who cared for her and to have children. By 1967 she had reached both goals.

The Tinning's first child, Barbara Ann, was born on May 31, 1967. Their second child, Joseph, was born on January 10, 1970. In October 1971, Marybeth was pregnant with their third child, when her father died of a sudden heart attack. This became the first of a series of tragic events for the Tinning family.

Marybeth

Marybeth Roe was born on September 11, 1942, in
Duanesburg, a small town located on State Route 20 about
ten miles south of Schenectady, consisting of 73.5 square
miles as a predominantly agrarian town bounded on the
north by Montgomery County, on the west and southwest
by Schoharie County and on the south by Albany County.
Duanesburg is the picture perfect little town that they could
make postcards of.

 She had one younger brother and together they attended
Duanesburg High School where she was nothing more than
an average student. Her father, Alton Roe, worked as a
press operator in nearby General Electric, the area's largest
employer. Marybeth once claimed that when she was a
child, her father abused her. During a police interview in
1986, she told one investigator that her father had beaten
her and locked her in a closet. But later during court
testimony, she denied that her father had bad intentions.

GE Building, where her father worked

"My father hit me with a flyswatter," she told the court, "because he had arthritis and his hands were not of much use. And when he locked me in my room I guess he thought I deserved it."

Ellis Hospital in Schenectady, New York

Though Mary Beth aspired to go to college upon graduation, it never happened. Over the next few years, she worked in a series of low paying, unskilled jobs that did not offer much of a future. Eventually, she became a nurse's aide at Ellis Hospital in Schenectady where she performed her duties in an adequate manner. In 1963, she met Joe Tinning on a blind date with some friends. He was a shy young man with a kindly disposition who had never been in trouble with the police. Joe was a quiet man who worked for General Electric, not prone to outbursts of temper and seemed to take life in stride.

The two dated for several months. The future looked promising for Marybeth, a good job a great man and plans for a beautiful future. In 1965 they married and started building that future.

Marybeth Tinning once said that there were two things she wanted from life- to be married to someone who cared for her and to have children. By 1967 she had reached both goals.

As an adult, Marybeth was a woman of average appearance. Photographs of her that appeared in newspapers over several years show a person who was attractive to the camera at times. On other occasions, she did not fare as well. She was 5-feet 4-inches tall, had blue eyes, blonde hair and a trim, though not a sexy figure. Marybeth kept her hair short and maintained a neat, proper appearance.

In almost all aspects, Joe and Marybeth were like many other young married couples in that part of New York. They worked hard, tried to make a decent living and build a better life. Except for one strange and persistent problem: Their children began to die.

The Web of Death

A mysterious set of coincidences surrounded the deaths of Marybeth's nine healthy children over a period of 14 years. It wasn't that no one had noticed that all of her children had died. Everyone noticed. But few people, very few, knew all the details of all the deaths. The Department of Social Services, the Medical Examiner's Office, several police departments, friends, neighbors, family and even the local funeral home had, at one time or another, registered their shock and disbelief at the odd calamity that had befallen the Tinning family. It is true not everyone thought it was a tragedy. Some saw the deaths as questionable and even made official reports of their suspicions. But in each and every case, no decisive action was taken against either Joe or Marybeth. There was simply no conclusive evidence that anything was wrong.

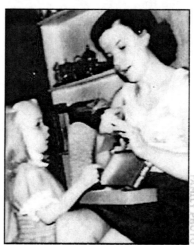

Daughter Barbara (left) and Marybeth
Tinning

Jennifer

First Child to Die

In the first five years of her marriage to Joe, the couple had two children, Barbara and Joseph Jr. In October 1971, Marybeth's father died of a sudden heart attack. On December 26th that same year, Marybeth gave birth to a third child, Jennifer. She was kept hospitalized because of a severe infection and she died eight days later on January 3, 1972. According to the autopsy report, the cause of death was acute meningitis.

Some who attended Jennifer's funeral remembered that it seemed more like a social event than a funeral. Any remorse Marybeth was experiencing seemed to dissolve as she became the central focus of her sympathizing friends and family.

At that time, most investigators did not believe that this death was suspicious because Jennifer was sick at birth and never brought home. The successive deaths of her father and her baby may have irritated Marybeth's fragile mental condition. Never a happy, well-adjusted adult and frequently described as "strange" by many of her friends and family members, Marybeth seemed to become even more distant after Jennifer's death.

Joseph Tinning, Jr.
Second Child to Die

The next 17 days would be a time of mourning and reflection as family and friends came to comfort the Tinning family. Joe was trying to deal with the death of his newborn child and at the same time, trying to comfort his wife who was emotionally drained from the experience.

One of Joe's coworkers commented that "losing a child at birth is in some way less traumatic for the father than losing a young child who has grown and bonded with you." 17 days later that theory would come to be tested.....

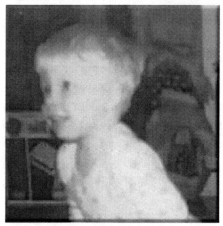

Joseph Tinning, Jr.

Thursday January 20, 1972, was just a normal day in the Tinning home. Marybeth was still mourning the death of her daughter, and Joe was back to work. But things would change later in the morning for the Tinning household. Marybeth took Joseph Jr., age 2, to the Ellis Hospital emergency room in Schenectady. She reported that he had some type of seizure. The emergency room was not too busy that Thursday afternoon so all the available emergency physicians jumped right in and focused on little Joey. The child was kept under observation for a time. When doctors could not find anything wrong with him, Joseph Jr. was sent home. Several hours later, Marybeth rushed back to the ER with little Joey. Unfortunately this time, he was dead. She told doctors that she had placed him in bed and returned later to find him tangled in the sheets and his body was blue.

Ellis Hospital

"He was taking a nap," Marybeth told detectives in a later statement, "it was close to his birthday and he had slept, taken a nap, slept unusually long. Unfortunately, I did not go in to check on him and when I did, he appeared to be having respiratory problems of which I did not cause".

There was no autopsy performed, but his death was ruled as cardio-respiratory arrest.

The death of little Joey had "very little impact on Joe Sr." His close friends said that, "Joe did not seem devastated about the loss of his son."

With the deaths of Jennifer and Joe Jr. the only child left in the home was 4 year old Barbara.

Barbara

Third Child to Die

Barbara and Joe Jr. 1971

Six weeks later, on March 2, 1972, Marybeth again rushed into the same emergency room with 4 1/2-year-old Barbara who was suffering from convulsions. Tinning told the staff that Barbara had gone into convulsions. Though the doctors wanted the child to remain overnight, but Marybeth refused to leave her and took her home.

Several hours later, like the incident with Joseph Jr., she returned with Barbara who was unconscious. The child later died in a hospital bed. The cause of death was brain edema, commonly referred to as swelling of the brain. Some of the doctors suspected that she had Reyes

Syndrome, but it was never proven. The police were contacted regarding Barbara's death, but after speaking with the doctors at the hospital the matter was dropped.

When police asked Tinning about this incident years later, she barely remembered it. "Had a daughter," she told investigators, "while we were sleeping, she called out to me and I went in and she was having a convulsion. I guess I don't even remember whether ... I think maybe we just ... I don't remember whether we took her by ambulance or whether we took her, but anyway we got there and they did whatever they did." A rare, little understood condition, known as Reye's Syndrome, was suspected in Barbara's death, but never proven.

"Had a daughter," she told investigators, "while we were sleeping, she called out to me and I went in and she was having a convulsion. I guess I don't even remember whether ... I think maybe we just ... I don't remember whether we took her by ambulance or whether we took her, but anyway we got there and they did whatever they did."

By March 1972, all three of Marybeth's children were dead. They had died within 90 days of each other, a highly unusual occurrence, even if it were Reyes Syndrome or Sudden Infant Death Syndrome (SIDS). The deaths came as a surprise to everyone because up to the time of their demise; Joseph Jr. and Barbara were healthy and active. Marybeth had always been odd, but after the death of her children she became withdrawn and suffered severe mood swings. Some people thought it must be some type of genetic disorder that was passed from mother to child. That's why people were even more surprised when in the following year; Marybeth became pregnant with her fourth child.

The Tinnings decided to move to new house hoping that the change would do them good. After looking at numerous homes they decided on a small apartment just across the street from St. Clare's hospital. A few years later a relative would comment that they felt relieved that the Tinnings decided on a place closer to the hospital.

Unfortunately this did not matter as the web of death was now to be spun in the Tinning's new home.

Timothy

Fourth Child to Die

On Thanksgiving Day, November 21, 1973, Timothy was born. Timothy was a small baby weighing just more than 5 pounds. Marybeth took Timothy home two days later. A staff nurse commented that Timothy was a normal little baby boy, and showed no signs of any medical issues when he was taken home from the hospital on the 23rd. On December 10, just 3-weeks old, Marybeth said that she found him lifeless in his crib. Again, doctors found nothing medically wrong and blamed his death on Sudden Infant Death Syndrome, SIDS, also known as crib death.

SIDS was first recognized as a disease in 1969. In the 1970s, there were still many more questions than answers surrounding this mysterious disease.

Today people ask themselves why the hospital didn't look more in-depth into the deaths of these children. When 4 children all die in the same household it *should have* thrown up multiple red flags.

Christmas 1973 would be a somber one in the Tinning's home. Marybeth was obviously distraught over the loss of her 3 week old son. A neighbor later commented that Marybeth was a grieving mother and her heart broke over the loss of little Timothy.

Joe thought their marriage was strong enough to survive the incident and the couple stayed together despite what happened. He was later quoted as saying, *"You have to believe the wife."*

Nathan

Fifth Child to Die

The Tinning's next child, Nathan, was born on Easter Sunday, March 30, 1975. But like the other Tinning children, his life was cut short. On September 2, Marybeth showed up at St. Clare's Hospital with little Nathan, only five months old, in her arms. He was dead. She said she was driving with him in the front seat of the car and she noticed he wasn't breathing. Again, there seemed to be no rational explanation for his death. The doctors could not find any reason that Nathan was dead and they attributed it to acute pulmonary edema.

Friends and neighbors were aghast. Five of Marybeth's children had died. Four of them were in her exclusive care when they simply stopped being healthy. It was horrible, scary, and incredible. And some would even say down right suspicious.

One of Marybeth's friends said years later, "I can still see his darling little face. His hair was so blonde, and with those big blue eyes and the smile he was the most perfect specimen of a little baby boy. He was just beautiful!"

Nathan Tinning

The Death Gene

The Tinnings had lost five children in five years. Having little else to go on, some doctors suspected that the Tinning children were inflicted with a new disease, a "death gene" as they called it.

Friends and family suspected that something else was going on. They talked among themselves about how the children seemed healthy and active before they died. They were beginning to ask questions. If it was genetic, why would the Tinnings keep having children? When seeing Marybeth pregnant, they would ask each other, how long do you think this one would last?

Family members also noticed how Marybeth would get upset if she felt she wasn't receiving enough attention at the children's funerals and other family events. Marybeth was a mother distraught "on the outside" but on the inside she was happy about all the attention that she was receiving.

Marybeth was showing all the signs of a condition called Münchausen syndrome by proxy. Unfortunately even though the signs were present, nobody recognized them. And because of that the web kept being spun in the lives of the Tinning's children.

Adoption

After three years of having a childless home the Tinnings decided to adopt. In August 1978, the couple decided they wanted to begin the adoption process for a baby boy named Michael who had been living with them as foster child. Around the same time Marybeth became pregnant again. But the Tinnings did not cancel the adoption. Instead, they chose to keep both children.

Some people wonder now if the adoption agency looked into the deaths of the Tinning's five previous children. While others wonder if the adoption agency even knew about them.

When family members heard about the idea of adoption some held concerns, while others figured that this child would be a healthy child as they believed that the previous deaths were attributed to a genetic issue.

Mary Francis

Sixth Child to Die

Then two months later, on October 29, Marybeth gave birth to her sixth child, a girl they named Mary Frances. For the first 2 months Mary Francis was a bright eyed bundle of joy. But, some of the family members started to worry. Some of Joe's coworkers would make comments about the fact that all of his had children died young and wondered if this would still hold true for little Mary Francis.

And just like with her other children, in January 1979, the baby apparently developed some type of seizure, according to Marybeth. She rushed Mary Frances to St. Clare's emergency room, which was directly across the street from her apartment. A capable staff was able to revive her. They saved the baby's life, but only for a time. On February 20, Marybeth came running into the same hospital with Mary Frances cradled in her arms. But this time she would not be going home. She died shortly after she arrived at the hospital. The baby, just four months old, was brain dead. The explanation was the same as the others. Marybeth said she found the baby unconscious and didn't know what had happened to her.

Mary Frances Tinning

"There is really nothing to say," she told investigators years later, "than I found her in her crib unresponsive. I believe Joe was there. I can't remember." When an autopsy failed to find a reason for the death, again it was attributed to SIDS.

Jonathan

Seventh Child to Die

St. Clare Hospital

Once Mary Frances was buried, Marybeth wasted no time in getting pregnant again. On November 19, that same year, she gave birth to her seventh baby, Jonathan. In the meantime, the Tinnings still cared for their adopted child, Michael, who was then 13 months old and seemingly in good health. In March 1980, Marybeth showed up at St. Clare's hospital with an unconscious Jonathan. Like Mary Frances, he was successfully revived. But because of the family history, he was sent to Boston Hospital where he was thoroughly examined by the best pediatricians and experts available. The doctors could find no valid medical reason why the baby should simply stop breathing. Jonathan was sent home with his parents. On March 24, 1980, just three days of being home, Marybeth was back at St. Clare's, this time with a brain dead Jonathan. The doctors couldn't help him this time. He was already dead. Cause of death was listed as cardio-pulmonary arrest.

Jonathan Tinning

By all accounts the authorities should have been notified by now. Seven of the Tinning's children have died. And there was still one more left at home, little Michael. Some of the family members say that they regret now that they did not take action back then to stop the killings. But, at the time nobody ever thought of Marybeth as a possible killer. But, some family members have commented that deep in their hearts they knew that Marybeth was somehow behind the death of her children.

Michael

Eighth Child to Die

Less than one year later, a pivotal event occurred in the Tinning household. The Tinnings had one child left at home, little Michael. They were still in the process of adopting Michael who was 2 1/2 years old and seemed healthy and happy. But unfortunately not for long. On March 2, 1981, Marybeth carried Michael into the pediatrician's office, then two and a half years old. He was wrapped in a blanket and unconscious. Marybeth told the doctor that she could not wake Michael that morning and had no idea what was wrong. When the doctor went to examine the child it was too late. Michael was dead.

An autopsy showed he had traces of pneumonia, but not severe enough to kill him. And just like with her other children, Marybeth Tinnings was not held responsible for his death.

Later on during an interrogation she described what happened to police, "When I went in, in the morning to get him up and so we could go to the doctors, he was not, I mean he was responsive to a point but he was very limp and so on and so forth and so instead of calling an ambulance, I went from our house...put him in the car, literally threw him in the car and went to St. Clare's or I mean I went to Dr. Mele's office and went in there and...By the time one of the doctors...I guess took me and they said that he died of viral pneumonia"

Something else was happening, only no one knew exactly what it was. After Michael died, some of the nurses questioned Marybeth's odd behavior

The nurses at St. Clare's talked among themselves, questioning why Marybeth, who lived right across the street from the hospital, did not bring Michael to the hospital like she had so many other times when she had sick children. Instead, she let hours pass until the doctor's office opened for business even though he showed signs of being sick earlier in the day. It did not make sense.

However, Marybeth's paranoia was increasing. She was uncomfortable with what she thought people were saying and the Tinnings decided to move again.

Michael Tinning

The Genetic Flaw Theory

Is Now Blown

It was always assumed that a genetic flaw or the "death gene" was responsible for the death of the Tinning's children. Since Michael was adopted, this shed a whole different light on what had been happening with the Tinning children over the years. The long-suspected theory that the deaths in the Tinning family had a genetic origin was discarded.

This time doctors and social workers warned the police that they should be very attentive to Marybeth Tinning.

Tami Lynne

Ninth Child to Die

On August 22, 1985, Tinning gave birth to her eighth biological child, Tami Lynne. The doctors carefully monitored Tami Lynne for four months and what they saw was a normal, healthy child.

On December 19, next-door neighbor Cynthia Walter, who was also a practical nurse, went shopping with Tinning and later visited her home. Later that night, Walter received a frantic telephone call from Tinning. When Walter arrived, she found Tami Lynne lying on a changing table. Walter testified that the child was not moving and she could not feel any pulse or breathing. At the emergency room, the baby was pronounced dead

On August 22, 1985, Marybeth, then 42, gave birth to her eighth child, Tami Lynne. Like all the other children in Marybeth's care, she was destined to have a short life. On December 19, next-door neighbor, Cynthia Walter, who was also a practical nurse, went shopping with Marybeth and later visited her home. "I stayed for a few minutes and I wanted to hold Tami," Walter later testified, "but Marybeth asked me to give the baby back, so I handed her back and then I went home" (June 25, 1987, Albany *Times Union*)

Later that night, Walter received a frantic telephone call from Marybeth. "Cynthia!" she said. "Get over here right now!" When she went next door to see what was wrong, she found little Tami Lynne lying on a changing table. "She wasn't moving," Walter said in court, "She was purple and I couldn't feel pulse or respiration. She was not breathing".

Walter tried to determine what was wrong, but there was nothing obvious. At that point, an EMS team arrived at the scene. They immediately scooped up Tami Lynne and sped off to the hospital. When Cynthia asked Marybeth what happened, she told her neighbor that Tami Lynne "was tangled in the blanket." At the emergency room, the baby was pronounced dead. There was no cause of death apparent to the emergency room staff, but since they were fully aware of the Tinning family history, suspicion quickly settled upon Marybeth.

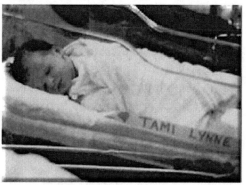

Tami Lynne Tinning

The next morning, Cynthia Walter visited the Tinning home to see if she could be of any comfort to Marybeth, who she assumed would be grieving over the death of her newborn daughter. When she entered the house, Walter found Joe and Marybeth in the kitchen. "They were sitting there, eating breakfast," Walter said later in court, "and I told them where I'd be if they needed me" Later, after Tami Lynne's funeral, Marybeth had people over to her house for a brunch. Her demeanor had changed noticeably. "She was smiling. She was eating, conversing with everyone there," Walter testified, "she didn't appear to be upset." Sandy Roe, who was married to Marybeth's brother, later testified that when she met with Marybeth after Tami Lynne's death, she didn't seem upset. "We spoke about Christmas," Roe said, "She never really talked about the death of the baby. It didn't seem to bother her."

But for some, the death of Tami Lynne became the final straw. The hotline at the police station lit up with neighbors, family members and doctors and nurses calling in to report their suspicions about the deaths of the Tinning children.

But police, who had suspected something was amiss at the Tinning household, went to interview Marybeth the same day. Schenectady Police Investigator Bob Imfeld questioned her about Tami Lynne's death and wanted details on how she died. "I know what you're here for," Marybeth told him, "you're going to arrest me and take me to jail" An autopsy failed to provide a valid medical reason for the death of Tami Lynne and as a result, her demise was listed as Sudden Infant Death Syndrome.

As for Marybeth's husband, nothing seemed to bother Joe. After each death, he would dress up in the same clothes and dutifully go to the services at the same funeral parlor. He would sit quietly at the wake without complaining and rarely make conversation with anyone. "There were things to make me suspicious," he once said to a reporter, "but you have to trust your wife. She has her things to do and as long as she gets them done you don't ask no questions".

The Genetic Factor

Dr. Michael Baden

Schenectady Police Chief, Richard E. Nelson contacted forensic pathologist Dr. Michael Baden to ask him some questions about SIDS. One of the first questions he asked was if it was possible that nine children in one family could die of natural causes.

Baden told him that it wasn't possible and asked him to send him the case files. He also explained to the chief that children that SIDS babies do not turn blue. They look like normal children after they die. If a baby was blue, he suspected it was caused by homicidal asphyxia. Someone had smothered the children.

Sudden Infant Death Syndrome (SIDS) was once responsible for thousands of infant deaths each year in America. Sometimes called "crib death," SIDS was a condition that was not well understood in the 1970s. Since that time, a great deal of research has been completed on this baffling affliction that takes the lives of babies in their cribs without any warning. SIDS is a diagnosis of exclusion. That means a determination of a SIDS death is usually made after everything else is ruled out. Doctors felt sure that SIDS was respiratory-related and that babies probably died from apnea, a sudden and unexplained cessation of breathing. It usually occurs in infants less than one year old and 80% of the victims are between two and four months old. Most experts do not believe that a baby will suffocate from being snarled in blankets and bed sheets.

Three of the Tinning babies were eventually diagnosed as SIDS deaths. This should have been a cause for concern since statistically, having two or three SIDS deaths in one family, is nearly impossible because SIDS is not and never has been, genetic in nature. Therefore, to have two occurrences in the same family is an extreme abnormality. Dr. Michael Baden, former Chief Medical Examiner of the City of New York, once said, "About three babies in a thousand die from crib death. The odds against two crib deaths in one family are enormous. The odds against three are astronomical".

Over the years, several physicians investigated the mystery in the Tinning home that led to the deaths of nine children. Hereditary factors were strongly suspected, though the unexplained death of Michael, the adopted son, lessened the possibility that there was some type of "death gene" being passed on to the Tinning children. Marybeth and Joseph also submitted to numerous medical examinations over the years to search for a cause. This proved to be of little value. Dr. Baden comments on the genetic theory in his book, Confessions of a Medical Examiner, "There is no known genetic disease that can cause sudden death in healthy children," he wrote.

Reyes Syndrome, an ill-defined condition that causes the brain to swell, was also suspected, though this explanation proved controversial and had little basis in fact. Reyes Syndrome produces noticeable symptoms. Family and friends observed Marybeth's children shortly before they died. With the exception of Jennifer, the babies seemed healthy.

"Just about everyone who came into contact with the family, the hospital, doctors, social service workers, was suspicious," said Schenectady Police Chief Richard E. Nelson to the press, "and communicated that suspicion to each other, many from the very beginning" (Feb. 8, 1986, *New York Times*). However, the problem wasn't that people weren't skeptical. The problem was that an exact cause of death for the babies could not be determined. Without a definitive ruling from the medical examiner's office a unified investigative effort from the police department could not take place. Dr. Robert Sullivan, the medical examiner of Schenectady was interviewed by author Joyce Egginton for her book on the case, From Cradle to Grave, "As I look back," he said, "the main problem is that different persons or agencies knew about every one of these deaths, but there was no centralized collection of information. It was all of us together...and all of us failed" (Egginton).

Neighbors of the Tinnings knew all too well the story of their dead children. "I knew she had lost five children and I had my suspicions," one neighbor told the *New York Times*,

"But who was I to point a finger?" In between deaths, Marybeth was frequently pregnant. When her baby was born, she was often seen walking down the streets, pushing a baby carriage, chatting with neighbors and fussing over the new addition to her strange and tragic family. Another neighbor once told a reporter from the *Albany Times Union*, "When the last child was born I asked myself, 'How long is this one going to last.'"

The Confession

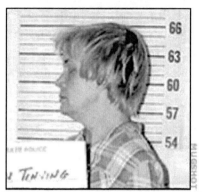

Marybeth Tinning mugshot, profile

After the death of Tami Lynne, police investigators from several departments met in Albany to discuss the bizarre Tinning family history. The deaths of the nine children, along with all the existing evidence in each case, were carefully reviewed. Medical reports were scrutinized, statements were reexamined and the available autopsy reports were studied. Even with the mountain of paperwork which spanned a period of 14 years, there was a consensus that a successful prosecution still could not take place without additional evidence. It was decided that Marybeth had to be interviewed again regarding the death of Tami Lynne.

Loudonville State Police Building

On February 4, 1986, Schenectady police detective Bob
Imfeld and State Police Investigator Joseph V. Karas went
to Tinning's home to ask her into police headquarters for
questioning. Of course, Marybeth was under no obligation
since there was no arrest warrant. The police told her that
her cooperation was needed if she wanted to clear up
suspicions about her child's death. Marybeth agreed, though
she later said she felt compelled to go with the police.
Shortly after they arrived at the state police building at
Loudonville, New York, police said they advised her of the
Miranda warnings and she agreed to talk to investigators.
At her trial, Marybeth denied she ever received these
warnings and said police intimidated her. "She said she
understood them," Karas later told the court, "She said
she'd waive them. She was willing to proceed without
them".

Marybeth spoke about her life as a child and growing up in
Duanesburg. She stated that she grieved over the deaths of
each of her nine children and denied any role in what
happened to them. With the exception of Jennifer, whose
cause of death was an infection, she assumed her children

died from SIDS or genetic problems. Concerning Tami Lynne's death, Marybeth said that on the night of December 19, 1985, she put her daughter to sleep in her crib like she normally did. Tami Lynne was crying that night, she said, which annoyed her because it made her feel like an unfit mother. She said that she watched television for a while alone. When she returned to check on the baby, Marybeth discovered she wasn't breathing. She said she picked up the baby and made an attempt to revive her. But nothing worked. Then she woke her husband and called for an ambulance.

The interview at police headquarters continued for hours. During that time, investigators Imfeld and Karas touched upon the deaths of all the children. Some events went back 14 years and the details as remembered by Mary Beth did not coincide with the known facts. But after so many deaths, it would be plausible that a mother could be confused. At about two in the afternoon, another State Police Investigator, William Barnes, who knew Marybeth Roe since childhood, joined in the interview.

For several hours she told investigators different events that had occurred with the deaths of her children. She denied having anything to do with their deaths. But police didn't believe her story. It was too much like the other seven deaths in the Tinning household, all of which occurred when Marybeth was alone with the child. And SIDS deaths only occur while the baby is in the crib. A baby does not die from SIDS in its mother's arms. In fact, picking up a baby is the only known way to prevent a sudden infant death. In all the cases, there were no other witnesses. Most of the facts available on each death had come from Marybeth. She told the initial story; she provided the much-needed details; she described the last moments of each child's life. It was all too convenient and there was no one to challenge her version of events.

When Mary Beth was confronted with suspicions over the deaths, she initially denied any malfeasance. "I didn't do it!" she repeated. But after several hours of persistent questioning, Mary Beth gave in, she broke down and admitted she killed three of the children. Though she continued to insist she never hurt most of the children, she said Tami Lynne, Nathan and Timothy were the exceptions. "I did not do anything to Jennifer, Joseph, Barbara, Michael, Mary Frances, Jonathan," she said to Barnes and Karas, "Just these three, Timothy, Nathan and Tami. I smothered them each with a pillow because I'm not a good mother. I'm not a good mother because of the other children".

"I did not do anything to Jennifer, Joseph, Barbara, Michael, Mary Frances, Jonathan, and "she confessed," Just these three, Timothy, Nathan and Tami. I smothered them each with a pillow because I'm not a good mother. I'm not a good mother because of the other children."

Joe Tinning was brought to the station and he encouraged Marybeth to be honest. In tears, she admitted to Joe what she had admitted to the police.

During the interrogation, police had contacted her husband, Joe, at his job at General Electric and he came to the state police headquarters. When Marybeth was allowed to meet with him, they had a brief conversation. Joe asked her to tell the truth whatever it was. She began to cry while police stood nearby. After a few minutes, Marybeth admitted the murders to Joe. "After 5 or 10 minutes," Joe Tinning later said in court, "Marybeth said 'I killed Tami' very low. She had to repeat it." Joe had no reaction to his wife's statements. "I had withdrawn into myself," he said, "I was hearing but I wasn't reacting". But investigators had also heard Marybeth's damaging statements. State Police reports written on the day of the interview describe the event: "[Joe Tinning] also related the circumstances of the children's death generally and then reported that during the conversation with his wife that day at Loudonville she admitted that she had killed their children and that now she is sorry" (New York State Police reports case No. 86-66 and 113).

At this point the interrogators then asked Marybeth to go through each of the children's murders and explain what happened.

Police called in a stenographer and together, while investigators asked questions and Marybeth responded, they compiled a 36-page statement. In it, Marybeth admits to suffocating three children but continued to insist that she never harmed the others. She told police that on the night of Tami Lynne's death, she was sleeping on the living room couch. "I was about to doze off when Tami woke up and started to cry," Marybeth said. "I got up and went to her crib and tried to do something with her to get her to stop crying. I finally used the pillow from my bed and put it over her head. I held it until she stopped crying." Then she took the pillow, she said, and put it on the couch to convince Joe she had been sleeping. "I screamed for Joe and he woke up," she said, "I told Joe Tami wasn't breathing...I did do CPR, stupid as it sounds, but I knew that she wasn't alive anymore." When she was asked why she killed Tami, Marybeth responded, "Because she was always crying and I couldn't do anything right" (Tinning).

At the end of the statement, Marybeth wrote: "I did not do anything to Jennifer, Joseph, Barbara, Michael, Mary

Frances, Jonathan, Just these three, Timothy, Nathan and Tami. I smothered them each with a pillow because I'm not a good mother. I'm not a good mother because of the other children. She signed and dated the confession. Marybeth Tinning 1-4-86 8 pm" (New York State Police reports case # 86-66 and 113). She was arrested and charged with the second-degree murder of Tami Lynne. The investigators could not find enough evidence to charge her with murdering the other children.

"Everyone Did Their Jobs."

After the arrest of Marybeth Tinning, there was a lot of finger pointing in the Schenectady community. There was already a great deal of media attention on the case and the story of the nine dead children was well known. It was reported in the nation's newspapers and the television show "60 Minutes" broadcast a segment on the case. *New York Times* reporter Amy Wallace wrote, "There were six autopsies, but never any signs of abuse. There were whispers and suspicions. But somehow no one not the police, the coroner, doctors, social workers or neighbors, not even Mrs. Tinning's husband-detected something evil in the strange pattern of deaths."

One of the biggest problems in the investigation was the lack of communication between the medical examiner's office and doctors who handled deaths of the Tinning babies that were not autopsied. Some of the deaths, like Barbara in 1972 and Michael in 1981, had a valid cause listed on the death certificate. If a death cannot be characterized as a homicide, then, theoretically, a crime has not been committed, and a police investigation is not ordered. "Everyone did their jobs," Schenectady Police Chief Richard E. Nelson told the press, "but when you have a legitimate cause of death, where do you go from there?" But some of the other Tinning children had died from unknown causes, which doctors listed as SIDS. Though police had made some inquiries in those cases as well, their investigation went nowhere. Some still wonder how much "investigating" was actually done in those cases. Just the mere fact that so many children died in the presence of this

mother should have caused enough concern to "require" a
police investigation.

Marybeth Tinning

Soon after Marybeth's arrest, police and the D.A.'s office
decided to take the investigation a step further. On May 29,
1986, under the direction of Dr. Michael Baden and Dr.
Thomas Oram, chief of pathology at Schenectady's Ellis
Hospital, the bodies of three of Tinning's children were
exhumed from the Most Holy Redeemer Cemetery in
Schenectady County. They were transported to the Medical
Examiner's Office for further testing. Defense Attorney
Paul M. Callahan told the press, "My client was bothered,
upset by them exhuming the bodies" He asked the court for
a postponement on Marybeth's appearance because, "She
wouldn't be in the best condition to be in court". But it
really didn't matter. Confusion over the location of the
gravesites resulted in the exhumation of the wrong corpse

in one case. The other two bodies were too decomposed for a conclusive examination.

 Children that die at a very young age in some cases cannot be embalmed due to their small veins. And this was the case in the Tinning deaths. So when the Medical Examiner's Office received the bodies they would have decomposed due to not being embalmed at the time of their deaths.

In the meantime, Joe Tinning, Marybeth's unflappable husband, told reporters, "I wouldn't like them to do anymore, but I guess that's their prerogative." One of the doctors that performed the autopsy on Tami Lynne, Dr. Oram, took notice of Joe Tinning's apparent detachment from his family. In a profile that he prepared on the parents of the dead child, Dr. Oram described the father as somewhat distant. "The father seems to have shown little curiosity in the circumstances of all these children's deaths," he said. "He has difficulty in remembering all their names".

The Denial

Marybeth Tinning was indicted for the murder of only one of her children, Tami Lynne. Police and Schenectady County District Attorney's Office felt that was the single case in which they had the strongest evidence. Her admissions on February 4 to police investigators were crucial and would certainly be persuasive to any jury that heard them. In December 1986, pre-trial hearings took place in county court to determine the admissibility of those statements at a later trial. For the very first time, the public would hear Marybeth Tinning's explanation of what happened in her household where so many babies had died.

Marybeth said the police had threatened to dig up the bodies of her children and rip them limb from limb during the interrogation. She said that the 36-page statement was a false confession, just a story that the police were telling and she was just repeating it. "They were telling me what to say." She told the court, "A lot of time the police made a statement and then I just repeated it. These gentlemen were telling a story and I just repeated it". She said that the police yelled and threatened her and any statements she may have made, were in response to that intimidation. "I was just tired," Marybeth offered, "I didn't want to go on. I knew what they were doing was wrong, but it would appear they had me in their clutches". The Albany *Times Union* reported that Marybeth "calmly responded to almost all of the questions...but she fought back tears when she testified about what she claimed was a police threat to unearth her children's bodies".

State Police Investigator Joseph Karas testified that Marybeth came to police headquarters voluntarily and was not under arrest at the time. "She said she'd talk but didn't want to sign anything," he said in court (Dec. 10, 1986, Albany *Times Union*). Karas stated that he read Miranda rights to Marybeth and she understood them. Another state police investigator told the court that after Marybeth confessed to killing three of her children, she seemed relieved that it was over. The stenographer who took Marybeth's statement on February 4, 1987, Margot Bernhardt, also testified that Marybeth was not forced to answer any questions and seemed to understand everything that was said to her. But the real drama came on December 16 when, for the first time, the world heard Marybeth's version of how eight of her children died, essentially in her arms, for no known medical reason.

Despite her efforts to block her confession, it was decided that the entire 36-page statement would be permitted as evidence at her trial

And The Trial Begins

Schenectady County Court

The murder trial of Marybeth Tinning opened in
Schenectady County Court on Monday June, 22, 1987. The
prosecuting attorney, John Poersch, had been on the case
since before Marybeth was arrested. During contentious
pre-trial hearings, the prosecution argued successfully that
the crucial statements made by the defendant on February
4, 1986 at State Police headquarters were not coerced and
would be admissible. Marybeth's full 36-page confession
would be available at trial. "Once you have heard all of the
evidence and assimilated it," Poersch said in his opening
statement, "you will come back with a verdict of murder in
the second degree against Marybeth Tinning, who
murdered her child by smothering it." Defense attorney
Paul Callahan challenged the prosecution to come up with a
cause of death for Tami Lynne. "That is going to be very
critical," he said to the jury, "How did this child die?"

The defence was using a very common tactic in murder trials. The trick is: it does not matter what the accused said it is still a burden on the prosecutor to prove the cause of death beyond a reasonable doubt. At the time of Tami Lynne's autopsy the doctors failed to provide a valid medical reason for her death and as a result, her demise was listed as Sudden Infant Death Syndrome. It was now up to the prosecutor to "physically" prove that a murder was committed.

Marybeth Tinning going to court

The medical testimony at the trial was complex, involving several doctors, all experts, who held different opinions on the disturbing tendencies of the Tinning children to die suddenly and without explanation. Some of the testimony helped the defendant. Other portions were extremely damaging. Dr. Bradley Ford, who examined Tami Lynne when she was an infant, advised the Tinnings that in view of their family history, a crib monitor should be installed. The device would sound an alarm if Tami Lynne stopped breathing. But curiously, for some unknown reason Marybeth refused. "The monitor was recommended," he told the court, "but the parents elected not to use it" (June 25, 1987, *Knickerbocker News*). Ironically, the doctor did not insist on the monitor because the baby was in such good health. Dr. Thomas Oram testified on the cause of death. He denied that Tami Lynne died from SIDS. "I'm saying sir, in essence that I came to the definite, positive conclusion that this child was smothered," said Dr. Oram to the court, "This would be the only thing that would answer all the evidence".

Throughout the trial the defense called several physicians to the stand to refute that allegation and to offer evidence that all the Tinning children suffered from a genetic defect. Dr. Arnulf Koeppen, a pathologist at Albany Veteran's Administration Hospital, told the court that it was his belief that Jonathan, the seventh child, had died from Wernig-Hoffman Disease, a genetic disease that attacks the spinal column. When pressed on that assertion, he was unable to state that Tami Lynne had that disease as well. Dr. Jack N.P. Davies, a well-known pathologist, went a step further. He claimed that the affliction that killed all nine children was unknown. "Frankly," he said to the court, "I think this may be a new syndrome, a new disease". It was a new syndrome that would late be known as "Marybeth Tinning."

However to refute defense claims of genetic diseases, the prosecution called Dr. Marie Valdez-Dapena, a nationally recognized expert on Sudden Infant Death Syndrome. Noting that Tami Lynne had a perfectly normal spinal column, she said that "it's highly unlikely that this is a case of Werdnig-Hoffman Disease." Rather, she believed that "there is a stronger probability that this was suffocation with a soft object, in light of the family's history" (July 8, 1987, *Knickerbocker News*). Following Dr. Valdez-Dapena's testimony, the defense was allowed to call further witnesses to refute the prosecution's medical experts. It became the battle of the doctors with both sides calling six pathologists, all who had different opinions on how Tami Lynne died. Dr. John L. Emerey had the most interesting observation. "I'd like to investigate the family," he said, "The ideal experiment would be to let her have more children and look at them biochemically."

In closing statements, District Attorney Poersch stood on the facts of the case and relied on the jury's common sense. "I don't think there is any question that the prosecution has proved this case," he told the court, "I don't think there is any other thing we could offer to substantiate that Mary Beth Tinning killed those three children". Defense counsel Paul Callahan appealed to the jury's sense of fair play. "Don't be led into the conclusion that there are inferences and innuendos that are proof that she may have killed Tami Lynne," he told the jury in his summation. "If she didn't cry at the right time, if she laughed at the wrong time, does that mean she is guilty of murder," he added, "or that she's a human being with emotions?"

But the jury could not help noticing one important point. Marybeth Tinning, who was accused of the worst crime a mother could commit, who had been labeled a baby killer and faced a life sentence in prison if convicted, had refused to take the witness stand in her own defense.

After 29 hours over three days of deliberation the jury had reached a decision. The panel later reported there was at least some initial confusion over the wording in the New York murder statute. However, once that uncertainty was cleared up, the panel quickly reached a decision. Marybeth Tinning, 44, was found guilty of second-degree murder, showing "a depraved indifference to human life." The jury could not agree on the issue of whether she actually intended to kill Tami Lynne. But her statements to the police were the pivotal factor in the jury's decision.

After the verdict was announced, Marybeth covered her face with her hands and began to weep. Joe Tinning was typically unmoved. "I can't really complain that they didn't think about it," he later told the New York Times of the jury, "they did their job, I just have a different opinion on it" (July 18, 1987, *New York Times*). Defense attorney Paul Callahan told the press he would file an appeal immediately. The appeal, he said, would be based on Tinning's epic 36-page confession to investigators on February 4. Callahan said the document should never have been admitted into evidence.

District Attorney John Poersch said he was pleased with the decision and Mrs. Tinning may have to stand trial in the deaths of some of her other children. "I can assure you this is round one," he said to reporters outside the courthouse, "I will see Mrs. Tinning and the defense again!" (July 18, 1987, Albany *Times Union*)

"I think we could have convicted her without it," one juror told the Albany *Times Union*, "but that was a great part of it. We went over and over it, and there's no way in my mind that I feel she gave it unwillingly." The defense claimed that Marybeth was intimidated by police and would have admitted to anything. But the jury disagreed. "[Police] gave her so many opportunities to say 'I want to stop, I want a lawyer, I want to use the phone," the juror said later, "but she never did that." The conviction carried a potential 20 years to life sentence.

Sentencing

On October 2, 1987, Marybeth was brought into Schenectady County Court for the last time. Judge Clifford T. Harrigan was the sentencing judge. Prosecutor John B. Poersch asked the court for a maximum sentence of 25 years to life. "This woman knew the consequences of all her acts," he told the court, "she is a wicked woman." Defense attorney Paul Callahan requested the minimum 15 years. When the judge asked Mrs. Tinning if she had anything to say, she read from a prepared statement.

Marybeth read a statement in which she said she was sorry that Tami Lynne was dead and that she thought about her every day, but that she had no part in her death. She also said she would never stop trying to prove her innocence.

"I want you and the people in this courtroom to know that I am very sorry that Tami Lynne is dead," she said. "There is not a day that goes by that I don't think of her. I miss her very much. I just want you to know that I played no part in the death of my daughter, Tami Lynne. I will try to hold my head high and accept the punishment that society and the court requires for the crime I was convicted of. I did not commit this crime but will serve the time in prison to the best of my ability. However, I will never stop fighting to prove my innocence. The Lord above and I know I am innocent. One day the whole world will know that I am innocent and maybe then I can have my life back once again or what is left of it."

Immediately following her statement, she was sentenced to 20 years to life, with shouts from the audience such as, "Baby killer!" "Bitch!" and more, she was taken from the courtroom and remanded to the county jail. She was eventually sent to Bedford Hills Prison for Women in New York.

Though the district attorney's office promised additional prosecutions for the deaths of the other children, it never happened. In August 1989, Marybeth was indicted for the murders of Nathan, who was six months old, and Timothy, who was 16 days old. However, charges were later dropped due to a lack of evidence. Tami Lynne was the only murder of which Marybeth was ever convicted.

Back to the courtrooms

An appeal on her conviction was made to the New York State Appellate Court based on the notion that Marybeth's confession was not voluntarily given. "Our review of the record," the court said in their decision, "leads us to conclude that the people have shown the legality of the police conduct. Defendant testified that she willingly accompanied the police officers for questioning and that before leaving home she spoke with her husband, who advised her not to call an attorney...further evidence in the record supported findings that defendant was not handcuffed, threatened or coerced, that she was free to leave...Accordingly, defendant's conviction must be affirmed on all respects" (People v. Tinning 142AD 2d 402).

What could have been the motive behind Marybeth's bizarre behavior towards her children? Some investigators believed she became enamored with the attention and sympathy she received after each baby's death. Some deep psychological need may have been satisfied by the consideration that friends and relatives displayed for her. At each of the funeral proceedings, Marybeth was always the focus of adulation. She was viewed mostly as a victim of some terrible unknown tragedy, which no mother would ever want to experience. This may have given her some unique sense of being someone special and deserving of the attention that everyone lavished upon her despite the morbid circumstances. These symptoms point to a rare and mysterious psychological condition called Munchausen Syndrome by Proxy (MSP). This affliction inspires the mother to physically abuse her child while showering the victim with love and care.

But the next question was, what about the death of Jennifer Tinning? She died in 1972 at the age of eight days, never leaving the hospital after birth. The cause of death was listed as meningitis. Dr. Michael Baden comments on this baby's death in his book, *Confessions of a Medical Examiner.* "Jennifer looks to be the victim of a coat hanger," he writes, "Tinning had been trying to hasten her birth and only succeeded in introducing meningitis. The police theorized that she wanted to deliver the baby on Christmas Day, like Jesus. She thought her father, who had died while she was pregnant, would have been pleased." The maternity ward nurses knew "Marybeth tried to induce the birth of Jennifer so that the baby would be born on Christmas Day, the reincarnation of her father in heaven."

Bedford Hills Prison for Women

Marybeth Tinning, now inmate No. 87G0597, is housed at the Bedford Hills Prison for Women in New York.

1ˢᵗ attempt at parole 2007

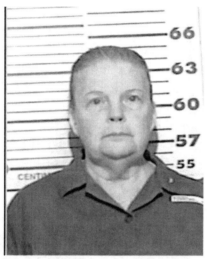

Marybeth Tinning

Marybeth Tinning, now sixty-four, appeared before a New York parole board on March 29, 2007 at the Bedford Hills Correctional Facility for Women in New York. It is the same prison that holds **Pamela Smart**, the New Hampshire school teacher convicted in the murder plot of her husband in 1990. Also incarcerated there is **Carolyn Warmus**, the blonde heiress who was convicted in 1992 of the killing of her lover's wife, a crime frequently referred to as the "Fatal Attraction Murder" by the New York tabloids. Tinning appeared before the three-member board who interviewed her about her crimes, her incarceration and her hopes for the future. It was her first application for parole.

Marybeth Tinning's bid for release had support from some surprising sources. Oddly, former State Police Investigator

William Barnes, who elicited her confession and whose testimony helped convict Tinning at her trial, stands behind efforts to have her released. "She is no danger to society at that age," Barnes said to reporters from Albany's *Times-Union.* "What harm is she to somebody and how much are you going to get from her by keeping her in?" Barnes was also joined by County Judge Clifford Harrigan, who sentenced Tinning to prison back in 1987. According to press reports, he allegedly wrote a letter of recommendation to the board that she be released.

At the parole board meeting Tinning said, "I have to be honest, and the only thing that I can tell you is that I know that my daughter is dead. I live with it every day," she continued, "I have no recollection and I can't believe that I harmed her. I can't say any more than that."

During the interview, the parole commissioners emphasized Tinning's apparent lack of remorse and her insistence that she simply does not remember what happened to Tami Lynne. "You were found guilty of causing the death of your infant daughter by asphyxiation. The victim was vulnerable and totally reliant on you for love, care and safety....you stated that during the interview that you could not believe that you would harm your child but could not recall exactly what occurred....you appear to have little insight into your crime and display little remorse. You have absolved yourself of responsibility."

The parole board takes several factors into consideration, including the inmate's understanding of the crime, remorse, responsibility and rehabilitation. Tinning failed on all those points. "Your depraved indifference to human life leads this panel to conclude your release is incompatible with the welfare of society. To release you would deprecate the serious nature of this crime...parole is denied."

The Schenectady County District Attorney's Office has not actively investigated the baffling case in many years. Detectives have long ago moved on to other assignments, pursuant to the demands of the office. But the statute of limitations never expires on murder. It is the only crime in which the books are never officially closed. However, since all the available evidence has been collected in the Tinning case and there are no new leads to follow, a prosecution for the remaining seven deaths does not seem feasible. And unless Marybeth suddenly confesses to what many investigators feel they already know, that she killed all eight of her children, one of America's strangest murder cases will remain unsolved.

Tinning next parole hearing is in March 2009.

2 attempt at parole 2009

Her only explanation for her grisly crime was that she was "going through bad times" when she committed the murder.

She was admonished by the board for a lack of remorse.

3rd attempt at parole 2011

In her most expansive interview to date, 68 year old
Marybeth Tinning, told the state parole board in January
2011 that she was a "messed up person" who smothered her
4-month daughter with a pillow because she feared the
infant would die.

"After the deaths of my other children ... I just lost it,"
Tinning told the board Jan. 26. "(I) became a damaged
worthless piece of person and when my daughter was
young, in my state of mind at that time, I just believed that
she was going to die also. So I just did it."

On Feb. 5 she was denied parole for the third time since
becoming eligible for release in 2007.

The Times Union obtained transcripts of the Jan. 26 parole
hearing at Bedford Hills in which Tinning reveals her guilt
in the murder more than ever before.

On Jan. 26, parole commissioner Mary Ross asked Tinning:
"This charge involved the murder of your 4-month-old
child who was smothered with a pillow, is this right?"

"Yes, ma'am," Tinning replied.

"Did you do that?" Ross asked.

"Yes, ma'am, I did," Tinning answered.

Ross later asked Marybeth Tinning what she thought when
her children were dying.

Tinning replied: "Two things that I wanted in life was to be married to someone who cared for me and to have children and, other than that, I can't give you a reason."

She said sudden infant death syndrome caused the deaths of her other children.

In the interview, Ross noted Tinning has certificates of achievement from nonviolence and anger management programs and that she now works for a chaplain. Ross and parole commissioner Jared Brown also cited letters of support for Tinning from people she has worked with in prison, as well as from Georgetown Law School, with some describing her as the "most loving, most generous, caring person that they have ever met."

At one point Ross asked Tinning, "When you look back at your actions ... what insight do you have into it or yourself?"

Tinning replied: "When I look back I see a very damaged and just a messed up person and I have tried to become a better person while I was here, trying to be able to stand on my own and ask for help when I need it, others when they need it. ...sometimes I try not to look in the mirror and when I do, I just, there is no words that I can express now. I feel none. I'm just, just none."

Tinning, noting she worked with AIDS patients in prison, said she would like to volunteer with such patients if released -- and that some places have told her husband, Joseph, they would be willing to use her.

She said she would live with her husband if released. He visits once a month but it is "getting harder," she told the board.

Tinning was also suspected of trying to poison her husband, but never charged.

On Feb. 5, the parole board's decision found Tinning's release would be incompatible with public safety and would diminish the seriousness of her crime.

She is eligible for parole again in January 2013.

The parole board's ruling stated: "This decision is based on the following factors: You stand convicted of the serious offense of murder in which you caused the death of your infant daughter by smothering her with a pillow. This was a heinous crime. You were in a position of trust and violated that trust by taking the life of an innocent child."

She is eligible for parole again in January 2013.

4th attempt at parole 2013

Marybeth Tinning, now 70

In her fourth bid for freedom, Marybeth Tinning, now 70, told a parole board she is held in prison by more than just the state — she is held in prison by her actions and her memories.

Schenectady County District Attorney Robert Carney, whose office prosecuted Tinning, said Tinning's latest parole comments relating to her memories, or alleged lack thereof, suggest she is still holding back information.

In her latest parole hearing, Tinning again admitted responsibility for the death of Tami Lynne, as she has since her second hearing. In her first appearance before the board, in 2007, Tinning denied responsibility, saying she could not believe she could harm a child.

At her second appearance, she explained her actions by saying she was "going through bad times." At her third hearing, she explained she saw herself then as "a messed up person."

Asked about the death of Tami Lynne at her most recent parole hearing, Tinning again admitted to killing her.

When asked about the circumstances though, Tinning couldn't answer.

"It's just — I can't remember. I mean, I know I did it, but I can't tell you why. There is no reason."

Asked if she remembered smothering her daughter with a pillow, Tinning responded that she didn't remember. "No. After the fact I remembered, but I don't remember why."

In her 2011 parole hearing, Tinning told the board she killed Tami Lynne because she simply believed she would die like the others, so Tinning just killed her. She'd lost it after all the others died, she said.

Tinning's memories then factored into a letter the parole board allowed her to read at the conclusion of the session.

In the letter, Tinning wrote she hoped the board members would find it in their hearts to allow her to go home.

"My actions and my memories hold me in a prison every day, whether I'm awake or asleep," Tinning read. "My heart breaks every day and I grieve every second. No matter where I am, I will live with my actions and continue to pray for forgiveness, and nothing will change that."

She then added it wasn't her suffering that was at issue. "It is both the loss of an innocent life and the suffering endured by my husband for my actions. I am very sorry."

Carney, though, pointed out Tinning's apparent two versions of her memory, her professed lack of memory regarding the death of Tami Lynne and then the reference to the memories that she contended hold her in prison.

"On the one hand, she tells them she doesn't remember what happened, but on the other hand, her actions and memories put her in her private prison," Carney said. "That seems to indicate she knows more than she's admitting."

Overall, Carney said, he doesn't believe Tinning has honestly come to grips with what she did.

Tinning's trial attorney, Paul Callahan, though, questioned the parole board's decision to keep her in prison.

Callahan noted a section in the parole transcript where the board cited her re-entry risk assessment, which was "low." Her criminal involvement was also "low" and history of violence at "medium."

"I think they're just — they just don't want her to be released, that's kind of what I'm seeing," Callahan said.

After her third parole denial, Tinning filed a legal challenge in court, called an Article 78. Court records indicate that it was filed in January 2012 and denied in June 2012.

The board's final rationale for keeping Tinning was similar to the previous ones.

"This was an innocent, vulnerable victim who was entrusted in your care as her mother, and you viciously violated that trust causing a senseless loss of this young life," the board wrote.

Release, the board wrote, would "so depreciate the severity of the crime to undermine respect for the law."

Elsewhere in the parole hearing, Tinning was asked about her other children, who all died before the age of 5. "Do you know why, what was going on?" she was asked.

"All I can tell you (is) in my papers and, in reflection, they died of other causes. It's in my paperwork, but they did not die by my hands."

"This was the only one?" she was asked.

"Yes, ma'am."

Later, by another board member, the topic of the other children was approached in a different way. If she had gone through such a terrible experience so many times with her other children, and then finally had a child that was healthy, why she wouldn't do everything in her power to keep harm from coming to that child.

"So, can you understand how we're a little perplexed that you can't provide any type of information as to why you did it?" she was asked.

"Yes, I understand," Tinning responded. "I have no reason. I'm not going to sit here and lie to you, make up a story. I just don't know."

Parole was denied. Tinning is next up for parole in January 2015.

In closing

No one can explain the strength of a mother's love. A woman who carries a child inside her for 9 months and nurtures them as infants….. Only to one day become their killer. No one can explain the strength of a mother's love…..

How to Report Suspected Child Abuse or Neglect

If you suspect that a child is being abused or neglected, you should call your local Child Protective Services (CPS) agency or the CPS agency in the State in which the abuse occurred. As you identify the appropriate agency for making a report, remember the following:

Not every State has a toll free hotline, or the hotline may not operate on a 24 hour basis.

If a toll free (800 or 888) number is available, it may be accessible only from within that State.

Federal agencies have no authority to intervene in individual child abuse and neglect cases. Each State has jurisdiction over these matters, and has specific laws and procedures for reporting and investigating. In some States, all citizens are mandated reporters by State law and must report any suspicion of child abuse or neglect.

Listed below are the toll free numbers for the States that have them available. If a number is not listed, or if you need to report suspected abuse in a State other than your own, please call:

Childhelp USA National Child Abuse Hotline
1-800-4-A-CHILD
(1-800-422-4453)
TDD: 1-800-2-A-CHILD
Childhelp USA is a non-profit agency which can provide reporting numbers, and has Hotline counselors who can provide referrals.

Bibliography Andrea Yates

"Andrea Yates," *Mugshots*, Court TV, 2003.

"Doctor: Yates Driven by Delusions," March 7, 2002.

"DA Looks at Rusty Yates' Conduct," Court TV.com, March 22, 2002.

Flock, Jeff. "Chilling Details of the Houston Child Killings." CNN.Com. June 22, 2001.

"Interview: Dr. Dietz," *Time*, May 19, 2002.

"Juries Often Spare Mothers Who Kill," ABCNEWS.com, June 28, 2001.

McCalope, Michelle. "Rusty Yates Bids Farewell to his Five Children." CNN.com. June 28, 2001.

"Mother Faces Jury for Drowning Five Kids," Court TV.com. Jan. 16, 2002.

Pearson, Patricia. *When She was Bad: How and Why Women Get Away with Murder.* New York: Penguin, 1997.

"Police Place Mother in Custody for Killing Six Children," *The Holland Sentinel Archives.* Sept. 5, 1998.

"The Prosecution's Big Gun," CBSNEWS.com. March 7, 2002.

Roche, Timothy. "Andrea Yates: More to the Story," Time, March 16, 2002.

Spenser, Suzy. *Breaking Point*. New York: St. Martin's Press. 2002.

Transcript of Andrea Yates' Confession. *Houston Chronicle*, Feb. 21, 2002.

"Trial of Texas Mother Begins Third Week," Court TV.com. March 4, 2002.

Williams, David. "Postpartum Psychosis: A Difficult Defense." CNN.com. Aug 8, 2001.

"Woman Throws Self, Twins into River," *Court TV online*, July 7, 2003.

"Yates Case Could Spur Changes in Texas Insanity Defense," *Mental Health Weekly*, April 1, 2002.

Bibliography Susan Smith

There are several books about Susan Smith and the crimes she committed:

Eftimiades, Maria. *Sins of the Mother*. New York: St. Martin's Paperbacks, 1995.

Rekers, George. *Susan Smith: Victim or Murderer*. Lakewood, CO: Glenbridge Publishing, Ltd., 1996.

Smith, David with Carol Calef. *Beyond All Reason: My Life with Susan Smith*. New York: Kensington Books, 1995. David Smith was married to Susan and describes his life with her and their sons.

Information about the investigation into the disappearance of the Smith children, Susan Smith's confession and her trial can be found in the *Spartanburg Herald-Journal* and the *New York Times*.

Bibliography Diane Downs

The Springfield (Oregon) Register-Guard newspaper, various editions, 1983/1984.

The Springfield (Oregon) Public Library

The Washington Post, several editions, with the most detailed story on June 12, 1984, page C1, entitled "The Mother & the Mystery" by Elisabeth Bumiller and Jas Saund.

Bibliography Marybeth Tinning

Baden, Michael M., Dr. (1989). *Confessions of a Medical Examiner*. New York City, NY: Penguin Books.

Boorstin, Robert O. "Schenectady Child-Suffocation Case Goes to Jury," July 16, 1987, *The New York Times*.

Cermak, Marv, "Autopsy Findings Awaited on Two Tinning Children", May 29, 1986, *The Knickerbocker News*.

Danzo, Andy - *The Knickerbocker News*.

"State Police Tapes Sought by Tinning Defense Erased", April 3, 1986,

"Tinning Murder Case Postponed, Accused is Upset by Exhumations", May 31, 1986

"Tinning Statements in Tot Deaths Bared", June 16, 1986,

Egginton, Joyce (1989). *From Cradle to Grave*. New York City, NY: Jove Books.

http://nysdocs.state.ny.us

Inmate Information, New York State Department of Correctional Services,

Mahoney, Joe. - *Albany Times Union*

"Court Papers Link Tinning to Killing of 3 Children", May 29, 1986,

"Physician: Kids Wanted by Tinning", June 17, 1986,

"Tinning Claims Pressure, Murder Suspect Takes the Stand", Dec. 16, 1986, "Tinning's Ex-Neighbor Tells of Vain Effort to Aid Infant", June 25, 1987, "Tinning's Fate Falls to Jury; No Verdict Yet Lawyers Make Final Plea", July 16, 1987

"Tinning Convicted of Murdering Baby Girl Faces 25 Years to Life, DA to Seek Charges in Two Other Deaths", July 18, 1987

New York State Police Case Reports: #86-66 and 113.

Pearson, Patricia (1997) *When She Was Bad*. New York City, NY: Penguin Books.

People v. Tinning [142 AD2d 402] Appellate Court New York State

Smith, Greg B. - *The Knickerbocker News.*

"Detective: Tinning Waived Rights to Stay Silent", Dec. 9, 1986, "Tinning Mood Swings Described", Dec. 11, 1986

"Tinning Says She Repeated What Police Told Her to Say", Dec. 16, 1986, "Tinning Mate Testifies Wife Admitted Baby Killing", July 3, 1987, Tinning "Defense Opens Testimony to Other Deaths", July 6, 1987

"History of Mary Beth Tinning, Family Studied in 6 Week Trial", July 18, 1987, "Gaps Remain in Official Handling of Child Deaths", July 24, 1987

"Tinning Proclaims Innocence as She Gets 20 Year Sentence", October 2, 1987,

Staley-Zimmerman, Debra S., Esq., Voorheesville, NY. Research assistance.

Tinning, Marybeth. Statement of Mary Beth Tinning dated February 4, 1986 at New York State Police Barracks, Troop G, Loudonville, New York.

Wallace, Amy. "After 9 Babies Die in 14 Years, Mother is Held", February 8, 1986, *New York Times*.

Wikipedia, the free encyclopedia

Look for these and other great books
By David Pietras

From "Mommy to Monster"

The "Daddy Dearest" Club

The Manson Family "Then and Now"

When Love Kills

The Making of a Nightmare

THE INFAMOUS "FLORIDA 5"

Death, Murder, and Vampires Real Vampire Stories

The Life and Death of Richard Ramirez, The Night Stalker
(History's Killers Unmasked Series)

Profiling The Killer of a Childhood Beauty Queen

No Justice For Caylee Anthony

A Texas Style Witch Hunt "Justice Denied" The Darlie
Lynn Routier Story by

The Book of Revelations Explained The End Times

Murder of a Childhood

John Gotti: A True Mafia Don (History's Killers Unmasked
Series)

MURDERED FOR HIS MILLIONS The Abraham
Shakespeare Case

The Son of Sam "Then and Now" The David Berkowitz
Story

A LOOK INSIDE THE FIVE MAFIA FAMILIES OF
NEW YORK CITY

Unmasking The Real Hannibal Lecter

Top 10 Most Haunted Places in America

40 minutes in Abbottabad The Raid on Osama bin Laden

In The Footsteps of a Hero The Military Journey of General
David H. Petraeus

BATTLEFIELD BENGHAZI

CASE CLOSED The State of Florida vs. George
Zimmerman THE TRUTH REVEALED

CROSSING THE THIN BLUE LINE

THE GHOST FROM MY CHILDHOOD A TRUE
GHOST STORY ABOUT THE GELSTON CASTLE AND
THE GHOST OF "AUNT" HARRIET DOUGLAS...

Haunted United Kingdom

In Search of Jack the Ripper (History's Killers Unmasked
Serics)

The Last Ride of Bonnie and Clyde

The Meaning of a Tragedy Canada's Serial Killers
Revealed

MOMSTER

Murder In The Kingdom

The Shroud of Turin and the Mystery Surrounding Its
Authenticity

The Unexplained World That We Live In

CPSIA information can be obtained at www.ICGtesting.com
Printed in the USA
LVOW06s0225241115

463965LV00014B/161/P